Acclaim for
In Our Backyard

"Nita Belles uses stories, statistics and history to illustrate the scourge of human trafficking that exists in America today. That this crime against humanity targets our children in such great numbers is an outrage that should not be tolerated. *In Our Backyard* is a call to action, and demonstrates that we can all play a part in eradicating human trafficking whether we adopt a faith-based, business, or any other approach. That it occurs with such alarming regularity on our shores should be a wakeup call for all Americans."

> —MARC KLAAS, President and founder of KlaasKids and
> Beyond Missing, frequent guest on CNN's Nancy Grace
> and other news networks

"The aptly titled *In Our Backyard* is superb, driving home that human trafficking occurs across town, not just across oceans. Belles compellingly calls for action based on the *truth* that every human life is of equal, enormous value—all created in the Creator's image. Belles shows how trafficking victims aren't 'illegal aliens'; they are ensnared migrants and, often, pimped U.S. citizens. Belles carefully documents how sex trafficking is inextricably linked to prostitution and pornography as fly paper preventing victim's flight.

"This book does as much as *any* to shed light on how *economic* forces—greed and demand, and even advertising—propel trafficking. *In Our Backyard* also demonstrates how business must do more than stop being an enabler in commercialized sex and supply chains; it must be an agent of slavery's abolition. Finally, Belles shows conclusively how the fight against today's slavery wouldn't have been started without Christian good works and won't be completed without them."

> —MARK LAGON, former U.S. Ambassador, and Director of
> the Office to Monitor and Combat Trafficking in Persons
> (TIP), former Executive Director and CEO of the Polaris
> Project, and Chair, International Relations and Security,
> and Visiting Professor, Georgetown University, MSFS
> Program

"This book is a "must read" for anyone concerned about issues of justice and compassion in this generation. Nita Belles takes on one of the most compelling issues of our time—human trafficking in all its various forms—and exposes you to the dreadful reality going on around us, as she gives hope-filled approaches as to how you can begin to make a transformational difference.

"Belles' careful research sheds much light on this troubling subject, but she is no arm-chair theoretician. She shares from her own personal journey of caring for those who have been trafficked with humble authority that will point a way for you to get involved as well.

"Sometimes books on this subject can understandably be filled with resentment and bitterness, because of such great injustice. You will not find that here. Though clear in exposing evil, there is no harshness in Belles' tone. At other times books like this can be filled with hopelessness and fatalism, because of the enormity of the problem. Not so here. Although you will read alarming global statistics, Belles' words are always marked by hope. Change can happen.

"Belles is working for change. You can too! I urge you to pick up this book. Once you start reading you won't be able to put it down. I couldn't. And when you've finished reading, join the ranks of those who are forming a modern abolitionist movement to eradicate slavery from your own backyard and to the ends of the earth."

—David Joel Hamilton, Vice President for Strategic
        Innovation, University of the Nations, Youth with a
        Mission (YWAM)

"Human Trafficking has become the latest buzzword in the Christian community but Nita Belles has done us a great favor. She not only addresses the sensational aspects of the problem in a clearly documented manner—she has the chutzpah to point out the elephant in the room that no one wants to talk about. The fact that many Christians are the customers, including pastors. 'Bravo Nita!' Thanks for your honest, prophetic, hard work!"

—Dr. Ted Roberts, CSAT CMAT, best selling author,
        pastor and clinical counselor, Founder, Pure Desire
        Ministries International

"A long time coming!

"For too long we have dismissed the cries of hopeless trafficked victims thinking, 'These things only happen in faraway places.' The reality is that trafficking is taking place right on our doorstep! Once you have read Belles' compelling accounts of the 'slaves of the trade' you will no longer be able to reject the inconceivability of something so atrocious happening 'in your backyard.'

"In this book, Belles gives a compelling, comprehensive account of the veracity of trafficking in the United States. The narratives are an eye opener—revealing the hardships and hopelessness of countless thousands of victims who are the commodity of this multi-million dollar industry. Shame on us!

"Belles, for many years an advocate for domestic violence victims, now takes up the challenge of raising awareness about slavery and the crumbling social fabric of a society that closes its eyes to the horrific lives of the men, women and children who endure the heartbreak of human trafficking.

"Her Christian perspective is refreshing and a challenge for all who feel a tug at the heartstrings. Will we rise up and let our voice be heard? Will we be the ones who speak up? Belles provides the facts. The decision is yours!"

—GABRIELLA VAN BREDA, Executive Director of World
   Impact Network, Board of Directors of Foursquare
   Foundation

"Wow, what a wakeup call to the church!

"Solomon wrote in Ecclesiastes 4:1, *Behold the tears of the oppressed; they have no comforter.* Nita Belles' *In Our Backyard* serves as a wakeup call to the church to *look* in their sanctuary, at their next-door neighbor, in the restaurant their worshippers will eat at on Sunday morning and throughout their community and *see* the tears of the oppressed.

"*In Our Backyard* is more than a simple wake-up call; it is also a *call to action* to become the shepherds that God has called each of us to be. It's a call to action to rescue, protect and comfort human trafficking victims. To stop human trafficking, good people will need to rise up, look and really see what is happening in their backyard, and then do something about it."

—PASTOR BRAD DENNIS, Director of KlaasKids
   Foundation's National Search Center for Missing and
   Trafficked Children

IN OUR BACKYARD

IN OUR BACKYARD

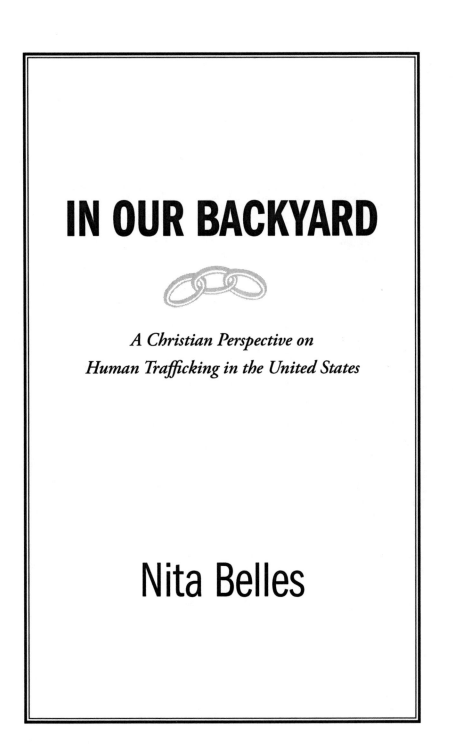

*A Christian Perspective on
Human Trafficking in the United States*

Nita Belles

Dedication

~

This book is dedicated to all the precious ones being used as modern-day slaves, to those of you who are sleeping in doorways, on mattresses or on the floors of garages, utility rooms, warehouses, and crowded houses and apartments, and other places you never wanted to be. It's for those of you who have given up hope of finding help and those of you with a shred of hope left.

It comes with a message that you are loved—by people you've given up on, by a God who loves you in the midst of your circumstances—and with a message that the church is on the move. We are committed to doing what we can and to petitioning God on your behalf for the rest. Yes, you are loved. Believe it.

Note From the Author

While all the human trafficking incidents described in this book are true, stories have occasionally been dramatized to convey the tragedy of human trafficking on a personal level. In addition, certain names and in some instances other identifying characteristics have been changed to protect victims' privacy and safety.

* Whenever a name has been changed to protect identities, an asterisk follows the name when it first appears. Out of respect, all victims' statements have been quoted verbatim. The author chose not to correct—or draw attention to—any grammatical errors made by those whose native language is not English.

Some of the material contained in this book is for mature audiences.

CONTENTS

Acknowledgments

After many months and even years of hard work, I would like to thank numerous people who have helped make this book possible. Thanks to my editor Linden Gross for encouraging me when I needed it and helping this project to its completion. Thanks to the many survivors, ex-perpetrators, government officials, law enforcement personnel and those who work with victims in rescue and recovery for your time and your willingness to be vulnerable in order to help others by sharing from your lives. Thanks to Carol Smith for your valued input, editing and support. Thanks to my family for putting up with me being endlessly busy and preoccupied with this work. A *huge* thanks to my wonderful husband Dan; without his unending support, editing skills, long days and nights of work on this book, and patience and love, I couldn't have written this book. Most of all, I give thanks to my Lord, Jesus Christ.

These three remain, faith, hope and love,
the greatest of these is love.
—1 Corinthians 13:13

May this book demonstrate that love in
helping to end the atrocity of modern-day slavery.

There is neither Jew nor Greek, slave nor free, male nor female, for you are all one in Christ Jesus.

—GALATIANS 3:28

Preface

If you're like many people, you probably believe that human trafficking primarily takes place in Asia, Africa and Eastern Europe with some potentially happening in South and Central America. This misconception is one of the reasons I have written this book. Human trafficking exists in every state and nearly every city here in the United States as well. Look hard enough and you'll even find it in our nation's small towns and countryside. In short, it's *in our backyard*.

I live in beautiful central Oregon. Our region consists of small sleepy western towns, cities and farming communities, with some of the seemingly safest streets in the country. Tourism abounds here, with our 315 days of sunshine, wide-open spaces, rivers, lakes, mountains and air that smells so good it should be bottled. Not surprisingly, this area attracts conventions and other gatherings, as well as some wealthy and even very wealthy individuals looking for upscale and resort living. If human trafficking can happen in my hometown, it can and does happen anywhere. No community is immune.

I began to study human trafficking while working on my Masters degree. The stories I read about it and have seen are the most tragic I have ever known.

"What can I do?" I asked God. The answer that came to me surprised me.

I had never written a book before—my gifts seemed to be in teaching, training and motivating. Those came easily to me. By contrast, writing a book was very difficult. God was asking me to do something not impossible, but well out of my comfort zone.

I bring this book to you from my perspective. I don't write this as the greatest expert or as the activist who has done the most. I am writing because the stories I've seen and heard have broken my heart.

I am a wife who weeps when she sees couples separated because of slavery; a mom who wants to wrap her arms around a hurting young person whose childhood has been stolen; a daughter who feels the pain of separation from her family along with the shame that prevents her from contacting them; a sister who knows the feeling of helplessness while watching a brother or sister suffer and not being able to help; and a friend who rejoices with her friends in love, laughs with them during joyous times, and cries with them during others, because sometimes that is the most loving thing to do.

More than all those reasons, the very root of my life is built on a relationship I have with God. When things have gotten rough in my life, when the rubber meets the road, I find myself leaning on my faith and getting strength from the place I've found to always be faithful: God is there for me every time.

This book is built is on that faith. It is my offering to God and to you. The information it offers may save some child, some young woman, some young man, as it encourages all of us to live out our faith in this fight against human trafficking.

What do I have to offer the victims of this modern-day slavery? I have met some great people along this journey to whom I can refer folks for help. And I have developed some expertise while studying and working in the anti-human trafficking movement over the past few years. But the greatest thing I have to share is a love and compassion given to me by a God whose love I can't explain and couldn't possibly earn. Because that never-ending love has been given to me, I can give it away freely. Does this cost me? Anything of value has a price tag. But the rewards in fighting this injustice far outweigh the sacrifice.

"Truly I tell you, whatever you did for one of the least of these brothers and sisters of mine, you did for me."[1] Jesus clearly communicated that we are serving Him by caring for others such as those trapped in modern-day slavery.

I can't be all things to all people. I wouldn't last long kicking down brothel doors and grabbing pimps by the backs of the neck with a "Listen here, young man!" But I can talk to someone about human trafficking, sit with a victim and listen to her, guide victims to services, write letters to law makers, and call the authorities when I see something that looks suspiciously like human trafficking. By doing these things, I can re-gift the love that's been so freely given to me.

This book is not intended to be an all-inclusive look at modern-day slavery in the United States, but a sampling to inspire you to uncover more truths about this outrage for yourself and others. I have intentionally not endorsed specific anti-trafficking organizations. Instead, once you realize how pervasive this tragedy of human trafficking is, I encourage you to get behind one or more of many great anti-trafficking groups and support it as a volunteer, supporter, or prayer partner.

I must admit I've hesitated to write up some reports of victims' experiences that are so horrific I fear you might be tempted to doubt them. But to give you the full scope of what's really happening in our country, I have gone ahead and included a number of them anyway. Unfortunately, the truth is sometimes worse than what you might imagine.

Chapter 1

Modern-Day Slavery: It's Everywhere

*All that is necessary for the triumph of evil is
that good men [or women] do nothing.*

—EDMUND BURKE

Sarah* carefully navigated the early-morning traffic to school in "Betsy," a silver 2003 Honda Accord with black leather seats and bright chrome wheels, which her parents had given her for her sixteenth birthday. Her parents had thrown her a sweet-sixteen pizza birthday party two weeks prior, at church after youth group. All her closest friends had come and watched as she was presented with "Betsy." A big sign on the windshield read "HAPPY BIRTHDAY SARE-BEAR!" Sare-Bear was her parents' endearing name for her and a reminder of how special she was to them.

The present, however, had come with conditions. Her upper-middle-class parents had given her just two months to get a job to pay for Betsy's gas and insurance. And despite Sarah's 4.0 GPA, her new car also came with a curfew and the insistence from her parents that they know where she was and who she was with at all times.

---

*Author note: names with asterisks after have been changed to protect identities.

The morning had not started off well. Sarah hated arguing with her mom, but lately her parent's rules had been getting under her skin. "With privilege comes responsibility," they said. But now they were even telling her what she could and couldn't wear. Just last week she had bought a shirt from Abercrombie that her Mom made her return because it was "too tight and too low." She didn't really want to be a bad girl; she just wanted to fit in with what the other kids were doing. Besides, she really liked that shirt!

As she pulled into the school parking lot, she saw her new friend Maggie* wearing the exact shirt that she'd been forced to return. Maggie not only had nice clothes, she had all the freedom she wanted. This was high school after all, the time to have fun. Why couldn't her parents be more like Maggie's?

"Hey Sarah!" Maggie was always so happy to see her, and seemed truly friendly. "How was your weekend?"

"It was good; my family went to the beach. I really like your shirt! I actually bought that shirt, but my Mom made me return it."

"Why? Was there something wrong with it?"

"No, my parents thought it was too tight. Maybe I should have bought a bigger size." In front of Maggie, Sarah always felt like she had to make excuses for her parents' rules.

"That's how these are supposed to be worn. Hey, I'll give you mine tomorrow. I'm going to the mall tonight and I'll get myself something new. Besides, I think this is a better color for you than for me. It will look so cute on you."

"Maggie, you don't have to do that. Besides, my mom would have a cow if she saw me wearing that after she made me take it back."

"Why would you need to tell her? Just leave it in your locker here at school!"

Before Sarah could say anything, Maggie continued. "Your parents seem really strict. I'm trusted to make my own rules. I don't have curfews; I do what I want, when I want to do it."

That sounded good to Sarah, especially after the way she and her parents had been butting heads lately. They said she was rebellious, but how could she not be? They didn't seem to understand her or her needs. They had no idea what it was like to be a teenager today.

The next day Maggie came not only with the coveted shirt, but with another one as well. "Here's the shirt I promised, along with this other one that I thought would look so cool on you. It will show off your curves. If you've got it, flaunt it!" They both laughed.

"I can't take both of these. I don't know how I could possibly pay you back," Sarah said. She had been applying for jobs at all the clothing stores in the mall as well as at all the fast-food places, but no one seemed to be hiring in this economy.

"Don't worry about it." Maggie winked at her. "There's more where that came from. Let's hurry before we're late for history."

Sarah changed into the new shirt after first period and ate lunch with Maggie that day.

"Doesn't it feel good to wear what *you* want to wear? You look so pretty in that shirt! You're doing the right thing by following your heart."

Their friendship grew. Maggie was so at ease with herself, a trait Sarah admired.

She loved how Maggie made her laugh. Even though her jokes were a little crude, Maggie was so much fun and her life seemed so much more exciting than Sarah's. Before long, Sarah confided in Maggie about her unsuccessful job search.

"I need to get a job to pay for insurance and gas for my car. Plus, I want to be able to buy some clothes to keep at school so my parents can't nix them," she said with a sigh.

"Hey, the work I do is really easy. I can totally set you up," Maggie offered. "All you have to do is go on a date with this guy. You'll have to make out a little, but it won't be a big deal. And I can get you twenty bucks for it, which should cover your gas for the week."

"Who is the guy?"

"No one we know. He's older and just a little lonely. You just have to pretend you really like him for a couple of hours. It's easy money!"

Twenty bucks to go out on a date? That sounded good to Sarah. Her parents would think she was at the school football game and she could still make her curfew. The guy was in his twenties and she'd only be with him for a short time. Besides, the idea that her parents would think she was at the game while she was earning some quick cash seemed exciting.

Slippery Slope

The date didn't quite go as advertised. The guy demanded more than just making out. Sarah was uncomfortable at first, but it wasn't like she had sex with him. She only got to 'second base,' as the girls at school would say.

As promised, Maggie was waiting for Sarah after the date. She soothed her friend's concerns and they had time to have a Coke before Sarah had to go home. Maggie mixed some vodka in hers, but Sarah declined. The date was fine, but she knew better than to drink and drive. As they chatted, Maggie shared her weekend plans, which included not just one date but two, and with different men, no less. How Sarah envied her newfound friend!

Sarah, however, had no idea Maggie wasn't just a friend, but actually what is known in sex trafficking as a "Bottom Bitch." In a pimp's stable (the group of girls that he sells), there is a continuous competition to be his favorite. The "bottom" is the most loyal, and has a higher status both with him and within the stable. She can do many things the other girls can't, such as arrange dates, collect money, and train other girls and recruit. Befriending Sarah was just part of the job.

Sarah's weekend crawled by. Comparing Maggie's life to hers made it seem even more boring. Sarah felt a little conflicted about what she had done on Friday, but at least she wasn't a "square," to use Maggie's terminology, like some of the other girls in her church. Sarah wouldn't find out until later that the word *square* is used in sex trafficking circles to define anyone not involved in prostitution.

At school Monday morning, Maggie said that Sarah had really been a hit with her Friday date, and that he wanted to get together with her again. They arranged for Sarah to meet him after school that Wednesday.

"You're so exciting to me," the man told sixteen-year-old Sarah.

His words pleased her, and made her feel like a real woman. She agreed to drive up to the butte in his car to make out again. This time she was more comfortable and even enjoyed herself. And she really enjoyed the fact that her parents had *no* idea where she was and what she was doing.

Over the weeks that followed, Maggie and Sarah became better friends, and Sarah continued to go on occasional arranged dates. She could afford insurance and gas for her car, had new clothes, and was leading a life as exciting as Maggie's. Besides, the lie she had told her parents about her new job was buying her extra time away from home. The increased fighting with her parents was unfortunate but worth it, because in addition to her new job, Sarah had a new romance.

Maggie had introduced Sarah to her friend Alex*, and they were now secretly boyfriend and girlfriend. Sarah thought about him constantly. She was in love for the first time in her life, and he seemed to adore her. He had introduced her to sex and loved her in ways she'd never even known existed.

"The fact that I was your first makes me love you all the more," he said. Sarah knew having sex outside of marriage was wrong but she was so in love with Alex, she knew one day they would be married. She felt that somehow this justified their relationship.

During the month they'd been together, he had bought her new clothes, perfume, music and DVDs. He told her that he had never met anyone like her, that she was special and their love was eternal. They talked about living a wonderful life together. No one had ever cared for her in the way Alex did, and she was convinced he was right about everything. She realized now that her parents didn't really love her at all. Their so-called love was just about controlling her life. His love showed her what she really wanted, not just what *they* wanted her to be.

Admittedly, he did sometimes hurt her. Nonetheless, she wanted to be with him all the time. She would do anything for Alex. She had recently come to believe that's what a person does when it's true love.

She knew there were other girls in Alex's life, but he told her that she was the only one he really cared about. He ran the "dating service" where Maggie "worked," he explained. "Business is business. I have to mingle with all the girls to keep them on the straight and narrow."

She guessed they were prostitutes, but after meeting them, that didn't seem to matter. They were just real people. Somehow they didn't seem as bad as she'd been led to believe. And as Alex said, business was business.

Over the next few weeks, her feelings for Alex deepened. He always did little things to prove his love for her, like the time he sent all the other girls away so they could share the night together in a nice hotel. She came close to getting caught by her parents, who thought she was at her friend Sally's house. The narrow escape made her realize that if she and Alex were ever going to have the life they dreamed of, she would have to leave home. She was prepared to do whatever it took to preserve their love.

Fake Love and Real Love

One day Sarah drove over to Alex's for their usual lunchtime together. "I have to move to Vegas and I want you to come with me," he told her. "I can't live without you, Sarah. I've never loved anyone the way I love you, and we will be so happy there. No more hassles from your parents and we can be together all the time."

They left for Vegas about an hour later, after ditching the car Sarah's parents had given her for her birthday in the school parking lot. When they reached Sacramento twelve hours later, they met up with some of Alex's friends.

"We need money, Baby. All the other girls are back in Seattle. I know you'll be with me in your heart, but I need you to do these guys for us."

Sarah was surprised, but she knew the game. Besides, no matter what, she and Alex were together. She would think of him while she was with the others.

The next morning, Sarah was still reliving the nightmare of the night before. She had heard of gang rape, but she had never been roughed up and humiliated as she had that night. Part of Sarah wanted to believe that she and Alex would soon have their life together in the big beautiful house they had talked about.

As she handed Alex the cash from the night before, Alex questioned her firmly to be sure she was giving him all of the money including tips. He tried to tone down his demands by saying, "That's the way it is in the business, you know that." And she did know that. Pimps always get 100 percent of the earnings. "Don't worry, Baby, we're going to be living the dream soon," Alex said. But despite his assurances that she wouldn't have to do this forever, she knew she had been turned out and was now a "working girl." She had no doubts about her new nightly duties. Her job entailed bringing the money back to Alex. A mere three months after meeting Maggie, a life of pain and pretending had just begun.

~

Sarah's parents never quit looking for her. They searched up and down the west coast, as well as in Reno, Vegas and Phoenix. Although they hadn't found any trace of their daughter, Sarah's mother still knew in her heart that Sarah was alive. One day the phone rang.

"Sarah's been found," the detective on the case announced. "She's in Las Vegas."

Though Sarah was grateful that the raid on the brothel where Alex had placed her had rescued her from the life, she wasn't willing to talk with her parents. She was embarrassed, knowing full well what an enormous disappointment she'd proven to be.

When her parents walked into the room at the Juvenile Hall where the now seventeen-year-old Sarah sat in the brown overstuffed chair with her head hanging down, she didn't look up. Sarah's formerly fit body was skinny, her skin was pale and sickly looking. Her pretty, naturally curly blonde hair barely covered the tattoo on the back of her neck where Alex had branded her as his property. Her mother knelt by the chair where Sarah sat with her hands covering her face in shame.

"Sare-Bear, I love you," her mom blubbered between her tears. "You are the most beautiful sight I have ever seen."

As they fell into each other's arms in sobs, her dad's long arms encompassed them both and the three of them cried together. There would be many decisions to make, many tough days ahead, but Sarah had just been reunited with her parents who had never stopped loving her.

A National Crisis

Sarah's story had a happier ending than most. She was able to get into a Los Angeles Shelter called Children of the Night, where young girls who have been rescued out of sex trafficking are provided with the services they need to recover from their traumatic experiences. She received, among other help, treatment for the venereal diseases she had contracted, counseling for her emotional scars, and a diploma when she completed her high school education.

Unlike Sarah, however, too many human trafficking victims never escape their horrific lives, partly due to the fact that many of us have no idea that this is even a problem in our country. It may come as a surprise to learn that the National Center for Missing and Exploited Children estimates that well over one hundred thousand children are trafficked yearly in America.[2] While many of these young victims are runaways or kids who've been abandoned, others are from what would be considered "good" families and have been lured or coerced into human trafficking by clever predators. "These predators are particularly adept at reading children, and knowing what their vulnerabilities are," says FBI Deputy Assistant Director Chip Burrus, founder of Innocence Lost, a project addressing child- and teen-sex trafficking.[3]

But human trafficking in this country doesn't just take place where sex is sold. Labor trafficking, which occurs on the streets, in homes, in factories, in fields and any number of other places, is also big business.

Authorities estimate that:

- There are 27 million slaves in the world today.[4]
- Human trafficking is the second largest—and fastest growing—criminal industry in the world.[5]
- About 80 percent of all U.S. trafficked individuals are female, about 50 percent are children.[6]
- 70 percent of those female victims are trafficked for sexual exploitation.[7]
- In addition to the 100,000 youngsters trafficked annually,[8] 244,000 to 325,000 American children and youth are at risk for sexual exploitation and sex trafficking every year.[9]
- Each year, between 14,500 and 17,500 people are trafficked into the U.S. from other countries.[10]

Admittedly, these numbers are guestimates. The hidden nature of the crime makes exact numbers difficult to come by. We all want to see human trafficking statistics because they help us get our arms around the problem. However, with these types of crimes, even those statistics obtained by expert researchers conducting studies with the greatest degree of accuracy possible under the circumstances become best guesses. Yet these studies help us understand that human trafficking is a problem of epidemic proportions.

How is it possible that all of this takes place right here in the United States, and yet we don't hear much about it? Somehow, we Americans have operated under the misconception this crime happens somewhere overseas in places like Bangkok, Thailand, where many of us have heard about children being sex trafficked. It happens in the villages of India, where slaves do backbreaking work crushing rock for sixteen to eighteen hours a day, and in Russian cities where young women are recruited and shipped to other countries.

Why Focus on the U.S.?

We don't think about the sale of human beings happening right here in America. If we consider the possibility of human trafficking within our borders, we assume that it's confined to Las Vegas, New York, Los Angeles and other large cities. Even many people who recognize that this is as much an American disgrace as an international one don't realize that this crime doesn't just occur in our big cities. Although human trafficking has certainly been discovered in large metropolitan areas, it can flourish in upper-class suburbs, rural areas and even in small towns like the one in which I live.

Our homeless teen girls have reported waking up in the middle of the night with needles in their arms. About a week later, they disappear from the homeless camps and no one seems to know where they've gone.

Human trafficking happens in upper-middle-class neighborhoods that attract people who travel or do business internationally and "invest" in domestic help, which upon arrival in America can become modern-day slaves.

In search of a cost-effective work force, resort communities, hotels and country clubs sometimes unknowingly hire agencies that are actually fronts for slave labor.

Where there are regular conferences, sex-trafficked individuals are made available.

Finally, as you'll read in Chapter Three, church elders have even unwittingly supported human traffickers.

That's why whenever God presents me with a reasonable (and sometimes, I must confess, not completely reasonable) opportunity to enlighten folks about the modern-day slavery that's happening all around us, I take it, because I know the extent to which this problem permeates our land. Its prominence here makes sense if you think about it. Human trafficking follows money. America, being the richest nation in the world, stands to reward human traffickers with some of the highest profits anywhere.

Many anti-trafficking groups have sprung up in the last few years, with the underlying belief that if we link arms and do all we can, we can eradicate this atrocity around the globe. Some have committed their lives to stopping human trafficking in Thailand, Nepal, India, Indonesia, Vietnam, Cambodia, the Netherlands, South Africa, Kenya, Uganda and other countries.

I applaud their efforts, and thank God for putting that call on their hearts.

I am reminded that each person, no matter his or her age or nationality, has the same right to safety and freedom.

Overseas, we may hear of a six-year-old girl in India whose fingers are literally cut and worn to the bone from rolling cigarettes, or a pre-teen boy in Vietnam who hasn't had more than one meal a day for months while he works sixteen to eighteen hours daily harvesting rice, or a twelve-year-old girl servicing twenty men a day in a Bangkok brothel.

We may know of children in America, like the six-year-old migrant boy in California whose neck and back are growing distorted because of the heavy buckets he's forced to carry to the cannery containers, or the pre-teen girl in New York who is forced to work sixteen to eighteen hours a day seven days a week cleaning house and caring for the young children of a wealthy suburban family, or a twelve-year-old girl in Las Vegas who is being advertised as "fresh meat" and is beaten and raped multiple times nightly by perverted johns.

I am fully convinced that God weeps for all those in captivity, whether slaves in a foreign country or right here in America. It is wrong for anyone to be enslaved no matter where it occurs.

It certainly broke my heart when I learned about what was happening other places around the globe.

But when I understood what was happening here, in this country where I live and this country that I dearly love, I knew this is where God was calling me to make a difference. I have lived my entire life here and had not realized that slavery still existed on our soil.

I had to do something.

Modern-Day Slavery

So what exactly is human trafficking? Why is it sometimes called slavery?

Human trafficking is the recruitment, harboring, transporting, obtaining or maintaining of a person by means of force, fraud or coercion for purposes of involuntary servitude, debt bondage, slavery or any commercial sex act in which the person performing the act is under eighteen years old.[11]

Earlier in this chapter, you read Sarah's story about a young Christian girl from a nice home being lured into forced prostitution. As sketchy as the stats are, we know that roughly 2,200 children are reported missing in the U.S. every day.[12] Too many of those kids wind up as human trafficking victims.

This issue of human trafficking is possibly one of the most important issues of our day, Marc Klaas told me during my interview with him.[13] Marc is the founder of KlaasKids, an organization he established in 1994 to give meaning to the kidnap and murder of his twelve-year-old daughter Polly Hannah Klaas. Having created a legacy in her name that would be protective of children for generations to come, he now works tirelessly to raise awareness about—and to help find—missing children.

Some—perhaps most—of the children in America who become victims of human trafficking are forced into the sex trade. In fact, according to President and CEO of the National Center for Missing and Exploited Children Ernie Allen, who spoke before the U.S. House of Representatives, "researchers also estimated that one-third of street-level prostitutes in the U.S. are less than eighteen, while half of off-street prostitutes are less than eighteen. With the explosion in the sale of kids for sex online, it is clear that more kids are at risk today than ever before."[14] Several runaway groups have estimated that as many as one in three teen runaways will be tricked into sex slavery within forty-eight hours of leaving home.[15] The emotional impact on these youngsters is devastating. One study found that 71 percent of trafficked children exhibit suicidal tendencies.[16]

Children are just one segment of the population of trafficked individuals in this country who are imprisoned—whether bodily or emotionally—often abused physically and sexually, and always forced to perform for hours on end for little to no money. If that sounds like slavery to you, you are entirely correct. Indeed, the term *human trafficking*, which we used to describe Sarah's situation, is simply a politically correct phrase for what is really modern-day slavery.

How can this happen?

Unfortunately, it's quite simple. There are people motivated by greed and profit who are willing to use others for their financial gain, regardless of the hardship imposed on the person being used. The fact that few of us suspect—or even believe—that it is happening here gives the traffickers an unparalleled leg up. Even when trafficking is exposed, the proof required to bring the perpetrators to justice makes prosecution of traffickers very difficult.

In our earlier history, slavery was legal—and even socially acceptable. However, in the 1850s, the slave didn't come without a cost. Purchasing a slave to work the fields or in the house, no matter how odious that now seems, was quite an investment, with the cost equivalent to about 40,000 in today's dollars.[17]

One hundred and sixty years later, the cost of a slave has diminished greatly. Some say the average price is about $100. When I interviewed one ex-pimp, he finished my sentence for me when I said, "The cost of a slave today is…?"

"Nothing," he asserted.[18] He knew from experience how little he'd paid to acquire sex slaves to work for him.

If we think of an item that might cost $40,000, most of us would first envision a vehicle. In doing some research, I found that you could purchase a new Mercedes-Benz C Class for under $40,000. If you bought a shiny new red Mercedes for $40,000, you would probably be careful how you drove it. You would wash it, maybe even by hand, and regularly give it the tune-ups it needs along with all the recommended maintenance. In short, you would look after it carefully to ensure that your investment was being maintained.

On the other hand, if you could get that same Mercedes for $100 or less, and you knew you could buy as many as you wanted at that price, you would probably simply trade it in for a new model or dispose of it instead of bothering to take care of it. That's exactly what today's modern slaveholders do.

Today's slaveholder reasons that it doesn't make sense to invest in the maintenance of a slave who can be replaced for a very small amount of money. If the slave costs the slaveholder a significant amount of time, money or hassle, the slave is discarded like a broken CD player not worth repairing.

This principle is grossly illustrated in the movie *Human Trafficking*. In one scene, a child sex slave in Manila has developed a high fever. Concerned about the life and health of her friend, another child sex slave in the same seedy brothel attempts to secure medical help for her pal by telling the pimp about the girl's condition. The next scene shows the pimp coming in, picking up the sick pre-teen, taking her outside the brothel, breaking her innocent neck and disposing of her body, as the first girl helplessly witnesses her friend's murder.[19]

Even though slaveholders in the United States may not murder their slaves, they certainly do not invest in their well-being. Food is scarce, often just enough to keep the slave alive. Medical care is almost non-existent. And as with the slavery in our country's past, regard for human life isn't even part of the equation.

One of the most popular card games in the Wild West was Faro, during which gamblers wagered money, livestock, and slaves. It was a common occurrence for a slave master to return to his home, pull a slave out of his or her quarters, and send him or her to work for the game's winner.

That hasn't changed. "Girls can get traded from a card game or dice roll," says an ex-pimp I interviewed. "You could lose a girl and a girl would have to go. I mean, if you're in a pimp situation with a prostitute, you should [be able to] say right now, 'Guess what you get to do, you get to go be with him' and I'm not talking about dating. 'You can be with him now for good.' You should have that much control in theory because of how you set up your life."[20]

Using people as commodities is what human trafficking—or modern-day slavery—is all about. So it's not surprising to find pimps advertising people like products in big cities and even in small town USA. Online listings make this even easier. In May of 2010 a Craigslist ad read:

Jane Doe* Visiting Bend May 4–6
If you are a respectful, discerning gentleman who desires a vivacious and attractive companion, please contact me for more details. I'm a sensual and vibrant woman who is 19 years old, 5'10", with an athletic body and intelligent mind. $250/hour. Screening required. Email or call/text. Please no calls after 10pm.

Although Craigslist suspended its "Adult Services" section,[21] there are plenty of other places on the Internet where pimps advertise the girls they sell with ads similar to the one above. One can only hope that the people who control those websites will wake up to the reality that they are, in fact, accessories to the crime. I would ask them—and you—to compare the Craigslist ad above with this slave auction flyer[22] from 1829:

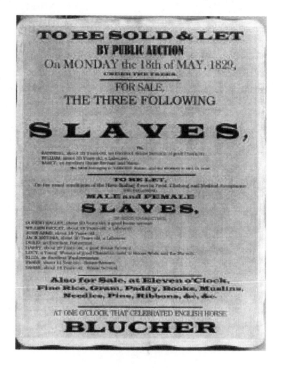

You'll note that in addition to the sale of slaves, commodities are also advertised on the poster. Similarly, one can shop for furniture, clothing, food, jobs and other items on websites selling sex.

Trafficking Victims Protection Act (TVPA)

Fortunately, trafficking victims—and those of us trying to help them—now have legal backing. In 2000, the U.S. Government began to recognize the need for laws to specifically address the problem of human trafficking. The Trafficking Victims Protection Act (TVPA) was passed. It has since been updated and will continue to be updated to provide better prevention against the crime of human trafficking and better protection for those trafficked into the United States, as well as for American citizens who have been trafficked. Victims now have legal rights as well as access to services. And those perpetuating these crimes within our borders or against American citizens who travel outside the U.S. for sex tourism or other trafficking crimes can be criminally prosecuted.

Stopping Demand

Ultimately, however, one of the main keys to stopping human trafficking extends beyond the legal system to all of us. In the universal law of supply and demand, if there were no demand, there would be no need for supply. Consumers insisting on manufactured or agricultural product lines that can be traced and proven to be clean of slave labor, for example, can reduce labor trafficking and help eliminate the sale of slave-produced products.

Sex trafficking is particularly dependent on demand. Without consumers viewing pornography online, without johns willing to pay for sex, there would be no need for sex-trafficked individuals. "The market for sex trafficking and sex tourism is just like a shopping mall," says Linda

Smith, founder of Shared Hope International and former member of the United States House of Representatives. "Buyers can choose from a variety of human products of various ages and colors, and as long as buyers continue to purchase this human product and facilitators support the market, the shopping mall stays open."[23]

Helping to Stop Human Trafficking

The question is, what are we going to do about this unconscionable situation?

We will probably each have a different answer to that question because God's divine wisdom created us all as individuals. As for myself, I am working to increase awareness about modern-day slavery happening right here in our country and to challenge other Christians to ask God, "What is it *I* am supposed to do to help fight this abomination?"

I can't answer that question for you, but I have listed below the beginning of many suggestions you will find in this book. Some will take short amounts of time, while others will require more effort. All will help the fight against human trafficking.

Volunteering even limited time, for example, to non-profit organizations effectively fighting the crime of human trafficking does more to help than you could possibly imagine. At our local chapter of Oregonians Against Trafficking Humans (OATH), which is an extension of the Oregon Human Trafficking Task Force, we couldn't do nearly as much as we do without the help of two of our volunteers.

Kristina is a quiet, busy young woman who, with her husband, owns and operates a successful and quickly-growing Karate school. They allow us to use that space for occasional meetings. Kristina helps me whenever I'm challenged with clerical duties (which is often). She also makes phone calls, oversees other volunteers, edits copy and even designs knockout posters and flyers. In the few hours a week she puts in, Kristina has even connected us with an accountant who donates services to our organization. She has a knack of looking for and tending to things that need to be done. Her deeds in and of themselves may seem small, but they add up to a huge contribution to our organization.

Another volunteer is Christi, a single mom who works hard to support her children and who would be a busy gal with half the things she does. She serves one of our organization's most vital functions by regularly sending reminders and supporting our "viral" efforts to get the word out about events via email and Facebook. When we had a large event last spring, Christi distributed the majority of hundreds of our posters. I kidded her that she's never met a blank space on a wall that she didn't think deserved a poster.

Christi and Kristina are strong soldiers in this fight against human trafficking. Countless numbers of people and leads come to us as a result of their efforts to spread the word about stopping human trafficking in our area. They're a vital part of our work. Their selfless efforts have helped to rescue victims and save lives.

While these two women are local heroes to me, even small, one-time acts such as making phone calls, allowing a poster to be hung in your business, or writing a letter to Congress can help make a significant difference.

Although not everyone can or wants to donate time, monetary contributions can be just as important. Both anti-slavery organizations and those groups that aid in the recovery and rehabilitation of newly freed slaves share a common and desperate need for funding. Educating the public about human trafficking, freeing individual slaves, and providing care and rehabilitation for survivors isn't cheap. The only way these organizations can continue their work is through generous donations from concerned people. Even small, regular donations of $10 a month help give anti-slavery organizations financial stability and can be more effective than paying hundreds or even thousands of dollars to participate in a short-term effort overseas.

The Bible repeatedly commends the virtue of generosity, and it also tells us that God rewards those who give generously and from heart.

Each of you should give what you have decided in your heart to give, not reluctantly or under compulsion, for God loves a cheerful giver.[24]

When you cheerfully give either in time or money toward God's work—including to anti-slavery organizations—you become a partner in the fight against human trafficking.

We often hear objectionable activities protested with the chant "Not in My Backyard." There is even an acronym—NIMBY—for that saying. However, the truth is that human trafficking *is already happening* in your backyard and mine. Until we acknowledge not only that modern-day slavery happens, but that it's occurring under our noses, and until we are willing to speak up when we see something that looks like it might be human trafficking, this atrocity will continue.

Discussion Questions for Chapter 1

I have indeed seen the oppression of my people in Egypt.
I have heard their groaning and have come down to set them free.
Now come, I will send you back to Egypt.

—Acts 7:34

1. How would you define human trafficking or modern-day slavery?

2. How might the tragedy that occurred in Sarah's life have been prevented?

3. What could you personally do to help your community become aware that modern-day slavery exists?

4. Find a recent news item that concerns human trafficking and discuss it.
    a. How could it have been prevented?
    b. How can you help prevent a similar situation from occurring in your community?
    c. Who can you have a conversation with to make a difference?

Chapter 2

What Would Jesus Do?

With God, I can do all things! But with God and you,
and the people who you can interest, by the grace of God,
we're gonna cover the world!

—AIMEE SEMPLE MCPHERSON

Given Kachepa[25], now a young man in his twenties, stood at his father's Zambia gravesite, to which he, his siblings and other family members had hiked through snake-infested, six-foot-high weeds and underbrush. The pain of missing his parents returned. Still, visiting their resting places had brought him peace. He had come home.

There was a time he had thought this would never happen. He thought he would never escape the Baptist missionary, Keith Grimes, who had taken him and other boys from his poor African community to the United States to sing in a choir and supposedly live a better life. And without Sandy Shepherd—an American wife, mother and devoted Christian—and others like her, he might still be enduring the brutal mistreatment to which he'd been subjected for so long.

The year was 1999. Eleven-year-old Given leaned against the wall, his arms wrapped around his knees. He was in the back bedroom of

24

the doublewide mobile home where he lived for months with anywhere from twelve to twenty-two other boys. Some, like Given, were members of the Zambian Acapella Boys Choir II; other members of other choirs were also working for the Teachers Teaching Teachers (TTT) ministry. Despite his exhaustion, along with the fear and hopelessness inherent in being crammed into such a small space, Given concentrated on trying to remain positive. But even with air conditioning, the Texas sun made the inside of the trailer home feel hot and humid, and seemed to intensify his misery.

Being tired and weak, he didn't feel he had the energy to shovel the stone-hard Texas soil one more time today. He and the rest of the boys from the choir had been so delighted when a few months prior, Pastor Keith had said, "You want a swimming pool? Wouldn't it be fun to have a swimming pool?" Little did they realize they would be forced to dig it themselves with shovels and picks. Today, as usual, they had been awakened at 7 a.m., made to go out and run, eat breakfast and then work on excavating the future pool. Hours later, despite bone-crushing fatigue, they had begun choir rehearsal. Given knew that they wouldn't get anything more to eat until they'd finished their five hours of practice.

The meal would be meager at best, consisting mainly of a cornmeal mush-like dish called Nshima. He knew better than to complain. Punishment for complaints about the lack of food or their extreme fatigue—or inquiries about why they weren't getting the schooling they had been promised—ranged from verbal assaults to the gas to the double-wide trailer being turned off, making it impossible for them to even cook their Nshima.

This was not the picture that Pastor Keith had painted of the lives he and the others would live in America when Given had auditioned for the choir in his home in Kalingalinga, Zambia. Pastor Keith had promised the comfort of shelter, plenty of food and a good education. Life in Zambia was so difficult, it had been easy for Pastor Keith to convince the locals that any life in America would be an improvement. Given couldn't wait. He was most excited about the opportunity to earn money, so he could help his family. Even though he wasn't the oldest, he somehow had always felt responsible for the care of all his siblings, especially his younger sister Doreen, and his oldest sister, Grace, who suffered from tuberculosis. He couldn't bear the thought of losing Grace to the same disease that had also taken his mom. He had to find a way to buy the medical attention she needed.

Given had been just seven when his mom died. Though he hardly remembered her, he still recalled the comforting smell of her body when she used to hold him close. He was too young to attend her funeral, but he often thought of her and tried to hold remnants of her in his heart and mind.

When Given was nine, his father died. "My world fell apart," he says. "I helped build my father's coffin and remember looking at him thinking he could speak." Given recalled going with his uncles and aunts to his father's funeral, and the metal and glass plate his uncle placed as a marker at the head of his father's grave. They did that so they would know where his father was buried when they wanted to return. Given had dreamed for years of going back to the grave, located two hours through the bush from the town, and visiting his father. He hoped his dad was proud of him, even though he hadn't been able to bring in as much money to the family as he had hoped.

As a child—and an orphan—Given looked constantly for any kind of available work. He broke stones and carried heavy loads to earn tiny amounts of cash. He carried purchases for ladies as they exited the mini bus. He sold paraffin for the cooking grills. He was able to buy food and shoes for his sister, but there was never enough left for the large sum it would cost to get medical care for Grace.

He took comfort in the services he attended at Highland Baptist Church. It was there that he accepted Jesus as his Lord and Savior, and entered into the relationship with God that sustained him through the hard times. Praying for hours at a time gave him the strength that he could only derive from the greatest relationship of all.

The Scam of TTT

Keith Grimes and TTT, who Given met in 1998, appeared to be the answer to his prayers. The seemingly gentle and trustworthy managers talked about other boys' choirs they had brought from Zambia to the U.S. They said that with the money earned putting on concerts at churches and schools, TTT would be able to fund the building of schools in Zambia. They promised that the boys who traveled to America with them would get a good school education, as well as a fair salary for performing, so they would be able to send home money to the families left behind.

This was the part that made Given the happiest. In addition to providing for his siblings while he was away, upon his return he could buy some land in Zambia and build a house where they could all live together. His big heart wanted more than anything to make life better for his family and this chance to go to America with TTT might be his only opportunity.

The village was buzzing with talk of the lucky ones who would get to travel to America with TTT. Given practiced singing constantly, even though he knew the odds were not in his favor since he was younger and less experienced than most of the auditioning boys. Still, he was determined to try his best. When he was told he was among the chosen ones, "It was like a dream come true," says Given. "They told us they were going to give us free everything—free clothes and money." What could be better than getting paid for singing about God's love every day and getting a great education, too? He hoped the paperwork would come through fast so he could go right away. His family needed money.

Although TTT had recruited and returned other members from Kalingalinga, Grimes' finely crafted web of deception, along with a clever campaign that discredited those who had come back, prevented Given from knowing the grim reality he would face when he came to America with them.

Sadly, his beloved sister Grace died before he could get to the United

States and start sending money home. He mourned her death and silently he prayed that no harm would come to any of his other siblings. He went to live with his Aunt Margret, but with six children of her own, there was not enough food, clothing or even blankets at night to keep them all warm, dry and fed. He helped her as much as he could, and earned money as best he could, but some days it seemed as if the cold and poverty was a dark cloud closing in on them. Still, Given felt God had provided a way to help them. News of his paperwork coming through couldn't arrive fast enough.

Finally, it was time to go to America. The flight was comfortable with plenty to eat. A tray of food all to himself? Little did he know that he wouldn't experience that sense of comfort again for a long time.

When they got to America, the boys sang in churches and schools, sometimes performing as many as eight concerts a day. Pastor Keith, who had seemed so gentle and kind in Zambia, was now cruel and demanding. Schooling was nonexistent, and Given soon experienced a new kind of pain and exhaustion. When the boys pleaded for more rest and sustenance, Keith verbally abused them for challenging his authority in their lives. They were also not allowed to question why they weren't being paid as promised. Instead, Pastor Keith gave them a list of scriptures, reminding them that they were there to be servants and were expected to obey their master. The hierarchy was both clear and coercive. Pastor Keith was in charge, and they were to be subservient. Complaints about their treatment were met with threats to return the dissenters to Zambia. The threats were real.

"I thought we were going to go to school?" a few of the boys asked eleven months into the tour. "When are you going to pay us for our work?" They were kicked out of the choir and turned over to the authorities for deportation. The message sent back to Kalingalinga with them would be that they had been disobedient, disrespectful and irresponsible. Sometimes when a boy was sent back to Zambia in disgrace, his family rejected him. The Zambian community was also more prone to believe a white pastor than an "ungrateful and lazy" Zambian teenager.

While on tour, the boys stayed with host families. Although the host families often offered them gifts, the boys had been forbidden to accept them. When the host families insisted they take phone cards, sneakers, Bibles or other gifts—or slipped gifts in their suitcases—the "contraband" would be confiscated during one of TTT's regular searches of the boys' personal belongings. Much later, it was discovered that Barbara Grimes Martens, Keith's daughter, had buried some of the gifts in the swimming pool hole the boys had been forced to dig. The rest of the gifts that the boys had treasured had been tossed in a dumpster.

In between concert tours, the boys were brought back to the crowded trailer in Whitesboro, Texas, i.e. the middle of nowhere. They were the only black individuals for many miles. Any hope of asking for help was dashed with the knowledge that people would believe the white American preacher over skinny black boys from Africa. That was one of the many things that kept the Zambian Boys Choir captive.

Though the boys regularly saw large sums given on their behalf in the church offerings that TTT collected at their concerts, the money never reached them and did nothing to improve their living condition or their treatment. They lived in a state of agitation, anger and exhaustion, whether performing or not. When young Given collapsed during one tour, Pastor Keith told him to stand and get ready to sing. "I'm too tired and weak," Given explained. "I am exhausted."

The pastor grabbed him by the shirt, stood him up and raged in his face. "I said, 'Get up and sing,' boy. Unless you want to go home, you will sing!"

Motivated by fear and the lingering hope of a better life for himself and his family, Given conjured up the energy to sing through the day's remaining concerts. He realized that despite the current hardships, he had no other options. TTT's leadership had told him that if the authorities questioned him, he was to say that the boys were happy, well fed, fairly paid, and wanted to be there. If he didn't tell them that, they promised to send him back to Zambia in disgrace. He would never be able to help his brothers and sisters that way. He had to be strong.

Things didn't improve even after Pastor Keith died of a brain tumor in April 1999. His daughter Barbara and son-in-law Gary Martens, to whom he had turned over the operation, were just as demanding and controlling as Keith Grimes had been.

Good Samaritans Take Action

The law, however, was starting to catch up with TTT. The boys had been told not to talk about TTT with host families, and TTT's leadership had told host families not to provide the choir members with any personal information that could lead to future communication. However, suspecting that the boys were being exploited, host families from previous choirs had tried to get help for their temporary charges. Phone calls and letters had been generated to federal, state and local authorities, and the FBI and Texas senators and governor contacted. The FBI determined nothing was wrong because they did not see any handcuffs or bruises on the boys. According to Sandy, one choir member even contacted "The Oprah Winfrey Show" to see if the superstar might draw attention to this case of modern-day slavery. None of these calls produced help for the Zambian boys. It seemed as if no one was willing to help. But the groundwork had been laid.

In the spring of 1999, Barbara Grimes Martens demanded the Feds take away the four boys who had protested their treatment for being a "physical threat." Although they were removed in handcuffs, law enforcement's investigation quickly revealed that the boys were not at fault. The Labor Department was informed and TTT was told to begin paying the choir members.

A lawsuit was filed on behalf of the choir members, prompting TTT to begin paying them, at least on the books. Behind the scenes, however, the Martens told the boys they owed back pay for housing, food, clothing, electricity, etc. Even though the Labor Department believed the boys were being paid in full, they were only given a very small amount of money, which was insufficient to buy the meals they were expected to purchase for themselves as they traveled from city to city.

The rescued "arrested" boys managed to get word back to Given that they had not been sent back to Zambia and had instead been placed in safe housing. That gave the remaining boys hope that they could get out as well. Finally, in January 2000, the boys demanded that Barbara Grimes Martens either pay them what she owed or call the Immigration and Naturalization Services (INS) to take them away. The INS was contacted and the boys were removed from the trailer. That's when the INS called Sandy Shepherd's church, and she was contacted and asked to help.

Sandy is an active and trusted member in her local church who regularly contributes to the choir, loves getting behind worthy causes and listens carefully to the Holy Spirit to hear how she can be a part of what God is doing. But she was busy with her own family's needs. Her daughter was in a major theatrical production at school and other pressing matters had rendered her busier than ever. Nonetheless, she felt she needed to house these boys so they wouldn't have to spend the night in a holding cell. Her mother's heart knew that after all they'd been through, they needed a place to stay where they would feel safe.

Sandy's sense of responsibility for the boys extended past that one night. After three months, she single-handedly managed to place each of them in long-term homes. Given went to West Texas to live and returned to visit in August 2000. During his visit with the Shepherds, the host mom sent Given a letter indicating that because of her health problems she could no longer house him. By that point, the Shepherds' last child had left for college, so they took Given in as their own. He has appeared in every family portrait since.

Given began eighth grade and worked hard to improve his English. He graduated from high school and the University of North Texas. At the writing of this book, he has begun his first year at Baylor College of Dentistry and is working toward his dream of becoming a dentist. Through the odd jobs he's held since starting high school, Given has sent money back to help his family on a regular basis. His earnings allowed his brother to build a four-bedroom house.

Sandy and Deetz Shepherd and other host families opened a school for the Zambian Acapella Boys Choir in Kalingalinga, making good on Grimes' empty promise years prior regarding education. That school still serves the community with high school classes.

A Dream Fulfilled

After what seemed like a lifetime, Given returned to Zambia with Sandy and Deetz to reunite with his siblings, family and friends. It had been eleven and a half years since they had shared time together. Given, now a grown man, looked very different than the eleven-year-old who boarded that giant plane in 1998.

After he'd sat for hours and days with his siblings getting reacquainted, Given set out to find his parents' resting places. He had been so young when his mother died. Witnessing kids and mothers interacting during all those stays in host homes had made Given wonder what his life would have been like had his mother survived.

He was grateful for Sandy and Deetz Shepherd. They had given him so much, and had shown him love in ways he'd never known in Zambia or with TTT. He loved them and thought of them as his American parents. In return, they, too, loved him like their own flesh and blood. But Given knew he had to find his roots. It was a part of who he was, and he needed to know.

The day he and his Aunt Margret found his mother's grave had a bittersweet flavor. Hand-dug graves, mound after mound covering a thousand acres, were overgrown with weeds that were especially high and thick in the rainy season. Margret remembered a mango tree being near her sister's grave. Finally, after digging through the grass on different mounds in the area near the mango tree, they spotted the small piece of metal with the correct number on it.

Given was relieved to find the spot where his mom rested. As he and Aunt Margret shared stories of his mom, he was surprised at the peace he felt. When he was a little boy, they had taken his Momma's body away to a place that he couldn't visit. He had missed her so terribly and dreamed in his mind of where she might be. Now he knew, and he felt the peace and the pain of closure.

Sandy Shepherd looked on at her son from a respectful distance. Her heart ached for him and the mother he had lost at such a young age, and yet was pleased that he had this moment. She knew this was hard on Given, but the experience was giving him a much-needed part of the puzzle of himself. As Given walked away from his mother's grave, he broke off the top of a large weed and grasped it tight in his hand. Taking it with him back home to America would be important to his healing. Somehow this weed from near where his mother was buried would remind him that he hadn't been abandoned or rejected.

Later that week, he set out to find his father's grave. This time, much of his family—aunts, uncles, brothers, sisters and cousin—joined him. Sandy also came to lend her support. The group walked for the better part two hours, deep into the dense bush where the threat of snakes and other creatures was very real. They also walked through cornfields, through weeds taller than they were and terrain so steep that they had to slide down in order to get through. Finally they found the area that Given and the others recognized as his father's burial site.

Given had now completed the trek to see his family. As he walked away from his Dad's grave, he broke off the top of another weed. Joined with his first bloom, these little pieces from where his parents lay would remind him that he was loved—by his mom and dad, by his families in Zambia and America, and by a God who had rescued him.

God is a God of second chances, a God who redeems. God is the father to the fatherless. God had certainly taken good care of Given, rescuing him from a life of poverty and disease in Zambia and a life of slavery in America, and redeeming him to a beautiful family, an education and a new life. The same God who was with him in Zambia was the God who sustained him through his enslavement and who continues to sustain him. Because Given has chosen to forgive TTT members, he now lives as a survivor, no longer captive to his victimization. As Given and his family walked out of the woods back to the village, he thought, "God is good."

God's Work

God *is* good, as are Christians who do God's work. But sometimes, despite our best intentions, we get misled. The Shepherds, for example, generously supported the Zambian boys' choir before they knew the truth about what was happening to the boys and where the money was going.

As Christians, we have all unsuspectingly helped to perpetuate human trafficking. We don't mean to. Most of us have no idea we're doing it. Those of us who do, abhor the idea that we are unintentionally contributing to modern-day slavery. But understanding that we are part of the problem can prompt us to be part of the solution. If we have the courage to look at how we have participated and we have the courage to challenge ourselves, we become an immense force for eliminating the human trafficking crisis that causes so much suffering in this country and around the world.

The first step involves simply becoming aware. As painful as it is, we need to think about Given and all those other people forced into servitude. Instead of turning away, we need to put our faith into action. We need to bear the pain and extend a hand.

Exodus 3:7–8 says:

> *I have indeed seen the misery of my people in Egypt. I have heard them crying out because of their slave drivers, and I am concerned about their suffering. So I have come down to rescue them from the hand of the Egyptians and to bring them up out of that land into a good and spacious land, a land flowing with milk and honey.*

Each one of you can do something, whether it's praying, talking to your neighbor about the issue of human trafficking, or donating time and/or money to help stop this atrocity. But we also need to look at how we let this happen, and why as Christians, we aren't all up in arms. And that means challenging the hierarchy that has encouraged our blindness.

The Targets

Trafficking attacks the vulnerable, primarily women and children, along with men like Mexican farm workers who lack social stature and money. It's easy to look down on those less fortunate than ourselves, especially when they're walking the streets in a sleazy outfit, cleaning the toilet or sewing the garments we wear. They're not like us. They're not at our level. So they're not as valuable as we are. None of us ever says it that bluntly, but our actions expose our hearts.

Sad to say, historically as Christians we have often followed the cultural interpretation of the Bible. Sometimes we have cited the "Book of First Opinions" and called it the Bible. There were Christians who were strong proponents of slavery in the 1800s in America.

"[Slavery] was established by decree of Almighty God...it is sanctioned in the Bible, in both Testaments, from Genesis to Revelation...it has existed in all ages, has been found among the people of the highest civilization, and in nations of the highest proficiency in the arts." Jefferson Davis, President of the Confederate States of America [26]

"The right of holding slaves is clearly established in the Holy Scriptures, both by precept and example." Rev. R. Furman, D.D., Baptist, of South Carolina [27]

Scary? These days that's scary, but in the 1800s it was the norm, the accepted cultural belief of the day and almost universally supported among Christians. If you had spoken against slavery in most churches (except for the Quakers, who took strong action to rescue slaves), you might have been ousted as ignorant of the word of God, and not following the Christian traditions. The church was equally backward when it came to women's voting rights. A brief look at history like this is all the more motivation for us to make sure that we're living according to the Bible's instructions. Social hierarchies that allow others to become invisible because of their color, their gender or their station in life are cultural values. These misguided values have been used throughout history to justify social hierarchies like slavery and the denial of women's right to vote.

"When bad things happen to men we say it's terrible, but when bad things happen to women we say that's just a cultural practice," says Lou de Baca, U.S. Ambassador at Large, Office to Combat and Monitor Human Trafficking.[28] Women and children constitute 80 percent of trafficking victims. Perhaps that's why modern-day slavery hasn't been challenged the way that it should.

The hard part about these judgments toward people is that they're often not even conscious. I am probably the most non-hierarchical person I know and yet I catch myself nearly every day thinking a hierarchical thought. That's how deep the conditioning goes. Even being aware of the tendency to classify people according to some internal pecking order doesn't stop it.

A story recently emailed to me wonderfully illustrates our tendency to pass judgment on others, and shows us just how misguided those judgments can be.

A seminary professor was vacationing with his wife in Gatlinburg, Tennessee. One morning, they were eating breakfast at a little restaurant, hoping to enjoy a quiet, family meal. While they were waiting for their food, they noticed a distinguished looking, white-haired man moving from table to table, visiting with the guests. The professor leaned over and whispered to his wife, "I hope he doesn't come over here." But sure enough, the man did come over to their table. "Where are you folks from?" he asked in a friendly voice.

"Oklahoma," they answered.

"Great to have you here in Tennessee," the stranger said. "What do you do for a living?"

"I teach at a seminary," the professor replied.

"Oh, so you teach preachers how to preach, do you? Well, I've got a really great story for you." And with that, the gentleman pulled up a chair and sat down at the table with the couple.

The professor groaned and thought to himself, "Great. Just what I need, another preacher story!"

The man started. "See that mountain over there?" he asked, pointing out the restaurant window. "Not far from the base of that mountain, there was a boy born to an unwed mother. He had a hard time growing up, because every place he went, he was always asked the same question, 'Hey boy, who's your daddy?' Whether he was at school, in the grocery store or drug store, people would ask the same question, 'Who's your daddy?'

"He would hide at recess and lunchtime from other students. He would avoid going into stores because that question hurt him so badly. When he was about twelve years old, a new preacher came to his church. The boy continued to go to services late and slip out early to avoid hearing the question, 'Who's your daddy?' But one day, the new preacher said the benediction so fast that he got caught and had to walk out with the crowd.

"Just about the time he got to the back door, the new preacher, not knowing anything about him, put his hand on his shoulder and innocently asked him, 'Son, who's your daddy?'

"The whole congregation got deathly quiet. He could feel every eye in the church looking at him. Now everyone would finally know the answer to the question, 'Who's your daddy?'

"This new preacher, though, sensed the situation around him and using discernment that only the Holy Spirit could give, said the following to that scared little boy. 'Wait a minute! I know who you are! I see the family resemblance now. You are a child of God.' With that he patted the boy on the shoulder and said, 'Boy, you've got a great inheritance. Go and claim it.'

"With that, the boy smiled for the first time in a long time and walked out the door a changed person. He was never the same again. Now, whenever anybody asked him, 'Who's your Daddy?' he'd just tell them, 'I'm a Child of God.'"

The distinguished gentleman got up from the table and said, "Isn't that a great story?"

The professor responded that it really was a great story!

As the man turned to leave, he said, "You know, if that new preacher hadn't told me that I was one of God's children, I probably never would have amounted to anything!" And he walked away.

The seminary professor and his wife were stunned. He called the waitress over and asked her, "Do you know who that man was—the one sitting at our table who just left?"

The waitress grinned and said, "Of course. Everybody here knows him. That's Ben Hooper. He's the governor of Tennessee!"

I love that story. We can ask God to help us change. We can ask God to help us begin to recognize slavery, as well as why it has been perpetuated.

In the end, it's really about neighbors helping neighbors. Jesus asked, "Who is your neighbor?" In the Parable of the Good Samaritan, he answers that. Jesus called us to love our neighbor as ourselves.[29]

Lately, however, I'm finding myself frequently asking a question: "If I'm to love my neighbor as myself, am I treating others the way I would want to be treated?" James 2:1 says, "Believers in our glorious Lord Jesus Christ must not show favoritism." For me, this is a challenge to leave the other person better than I found him or her.

Doing What God Asks

That's where the Holy Spirit comes in—to lead us and guide us into the things we are to do. I *can* do the things God asks of me day by day. And God *will* ask. That doesn't mean I obey perfectly every time, but failing means there is forgiveness available from a God who encourages me to keep trying.

Challenging our hierarchical assumptions helps remove our blinders and accept those whose lives are not what we would wish for our loved ones and ourselves. We sometimes make a point of not looking at the sex-trafficked individual with her short skirt and makeup who is probably packing STDs, or at the stooped farm worker laboring in the field. Instead, we pass those people by. But Jesus says those are the very people who are our neighbors.

Jesus loved those whom the rest of society had cast out as low-lifes. Once when the disciples were away and Jesus was by himself, he began a conversation with a woman at a well. According to the cultural values of the day, he should not have been talking to a woman, especially not a Samaritan. Some of you may know that in Jesus' time women were only marginally higher on the scale of hierarchy than farm animals but markedly lower than men. The fact that she was a loose woman dropped her even further down that hierarchical scale. The Bible even notes that Jews did not associate with Samaritans. Jesus said, "You have had five husbands and the man you are with now is not your husband."[30] But he treated her as a person worthy of his consideration, which is how he treated everyone, and even talked with her about spiritual matters. This was unheard of in that culture. Women weren't educated in spiritual things. If they had a question, they were to ask their husbands when they got home.

When Jesus says to the Samaritan, "Woman, believe me,"[31] that word *woman* was the same word he used to address his own mother at the wedding in Cana. He respected this woman whom everyone else had tossed aside as not in their realm of decency, not good enough to be their friend.

The woman he spoke with went on to convert a village. Tongue in cheek here, but I'm pretty sure Jesus knew what he was doing.

Jesus knew how to love intentionally. Jesus' life and ministry wasn't just *talking* about love, or talking about how to live and monitoring to see that his disciples obeyed the rules. Jesus intentionally lived love in his daily encounters.

I try to do that. And sometimes, by the grace of God, I actually succeed. It's a daily battle and choice. However, there are situations when I wish with all my heart I could do more.

For example, on Christmas Eve last year as I was scurrying around with my last minute preparations for the big holiday, I couldn't help but think, *What about those being sexually exploited in a brothel tonight? What about the man who buys a sex slave tonight as a gift to himself for Christmas, never mind that the woman he's buying is a real human being who hides the tears of pain under a hard surface because she'd like nothing better than to be home with her family, but is too ashamed of what she's become to even phone them? How can I help?*

James 2:13 says, "Mercy triumphs over judgment." It goes on to explain that faith is made complete by what we do. James isn't saying faith isn't important, he is just saying that faith without works is hypocritical. Protecting those who need to be protected, like those who are being trafficked, is near to the heart of God.

No one in history better typifies this than Harriet Tubman.[32] Born into a Maryland slave family in the early 1820s, she carried scars on the back of her neck from the whippings she sustained as a child from the various masters for whom she worked. At age twelve, she refused to help tie up a slave who had tried to escape. The overseer threw a metal weight at her, which hit her in the head. The skull fracture she sustained would cause her to live the rest of her life with her head drooped forward and her mouth often hanging open. She would fall asleep in the middle of things for no apparent reason and was regularly called *stupid*.[33] To those who owned her, she was damaged, devalued property, not a person.

It was after the time she sustained the head injury that her faith became real to her. As an illiterate child, her mother had told her Bible stories. Tubman acquired a passionate faith in God. She rejected the white people's interpretations of scripture urging slaves to be obedient and justifying slavery as God-ordained, instead finding guidance in the Old Testament tales of deliverance. [34]

It was by this relational interaction with and dependence on the Lord that she lived for God throughout her life. Perhaps because of this, Tubman lived a life of love and was able to value the person above her disagreements or even their abuse of her.

In 1849, she heard the Lord's voice warning her to flee northward.[35] Guided by the Holy Spirit and narrowly escaping capture, she made good on her escape only to find herself alone and lonely for family and friends. There was no one to help her, none of her own folk to share her joy. Her entire family, everyone she knew, had remained behind in slavery. She made a promise to herself that with the Lord's help, she would make a home for her family in the north and help bring them to safety. "Oh, how I prayed then, lying on the cold, damp ground, 'Oh, dear Lord, I ain't got no friend but you. Come to my help, Lord, for I'm in trouble!'"[36]

She would use her contacts and hard-won knowledge to bring others to freedom. Night and day she worked, saving pennies. When she had enough money, off she slipped from her home to rescue slaves and pilot them north. She returned to the south nineteen times, "bold to the point of brazenness," they said.[37] She delivered hundreds—and some say indirectly thousands—of slaves. She was so successful that a rumored $40,000 reward was offered for her capture, dead or alive.[38]

That was a huge sum in those days. But slavery then, as slavery now, is about money. And Harriet was really raising havoc with the slaveholders' wallets. Many times Tubman experienced a narrow escape. Always the Lord sent help. Once she had to lie wet in a swamp. Another time, she had to bury herself in a potato field.[39] But deliverance always came, sometimes through a friend on the underground railway, sometimes through her own wits.

No matter how she escaped, she *always* gave the Lord the credit. As biographer Sarah Bradford wrote, "These sudden deliverances never seemed to strike her as at all strange or mysterious; her prayer was the prayer of faith, and she *expected* an answer... When surprise was expressed at her courage and daring, or at her unexpected deliverances, she would always reply: "Don't, I tell you, Missus, 'twan't *me*, 'twas *de Lord!*'"[40]

Her boldness to lead slaves out of slavery earned her the nickname Moses,[41] stemming from Exodus 25. She believed she had been called by God to help her people, and once told an interviewer, "Now do you suppose he wanted me to do this just for a day or a week? No! The Lord who told me to take care of my people meant me to do it just so long as I live, and so I do what he told me to do."[42]

Though she was impoverished in her old age, her spirit remained unquenchable, and the God she trusted did not disappoint her. Her life is a powerful vindication of step-by-step trust in and obedience to the Lord. She was a person who dared to love her fellow human being unconditionally, even when she could have paid for that love with her life.

Might I suggest that we follow in the path of this young girl who was often called *stupid?* A girl who had no choices about whose slave she was. She was willing to overcome any and all obstacles to obtain freedom for herself and others. She then used past obstacles as stepping stones to accomplish what God had directed. She was courageous in obedience to God and lived an extraordinary life because of it. She had a love for others and faith to believe in the best for them. Signs and wonders led her and followed her life as she walked in obedience to Christ.

Might I suggest we follow in the path of Rahab the prostitute? This young woman, born into a life of compromise, loved God and her family, and not only wanted more for them, but also wanted to be on God's side. She unselfishly protected those she knew had been sent from God and risked her life for them. Ironically, she and her family were saved in the end because she was considered righteous.[43] A righteous prostitute? How did *that* happen? God was not ashamed to be linked to Rahab, the prostitute. She was in the lineage of Jesus. If God ordains who our mother and fathers are, certainly a prostitute being in the lineage of Jesus was one of God's intentions.

We serve a God who loves all equally, even those with a different station in life, and commands us to love in the same way. God obviously knew more about Rahab than the fact that she was a prostitute.

And finally, might I suggest we follow in the path of Jesus? He didn't care about the social ramifications of talking to a woman with a questionable reputation. [44] Instead he loved, respected and believed in her and knew what she was capable of, even though his own disciples thought he might have slipped up simply by talking with her. Because he was committed to live a life of righteousness rather than religion, he freed her to change her entire village. And 2,000 years later, we are still talking about that and hoping to follow His example.

For me, working to end modern-day slavery is not even a matter of fighting for rights for the disenfranchised, but rather for righteousness. This is the right thing to do. How do I do something to help bring modern-day slavery to an end? I try to start in my heart and on my knees, with the Lord, every day.

What About You?

Has God called you to join in the battle, even in what you might consider a small way? If so, then it's time to get involved in the fight—today!

Thousands of years ago, a simple shepherd named Moses heard a call from God very much like the one placed in Sandy Shepherd's heart when she took Given Kachepa into her home after his atrocious experience with the boys' choir. Like Sandy Shepherd, Moses had every reason to believe he wasn't the person God needed to help bring freedom to the enslaved. But God, who knew Moses' heart and capabilities better than anyone, knew who was best for the job.

Why do you suppose God sent Moses, a simple man, to bring the Israelites out of Egypt, a job that an all-powerful God could easily have done in an instant and with no human help? God was more than capable of stepping in and intervening on behalf of the Israelite slaves in Egypt, but has clearly demonstrated throughout history that the chosen vessels of change are godly men and women, people who see what needs to be changed and who, with God's help, summon the courage to speak up and do what needs to be done.

That held true during the time of the Israelites' captivity in Egypt, true during the abolitionist movements of the seventeenth through nineteenth centuries, and, I believe, holds true today. I believe God recognizes the suffering of modern-day slaves at the hands of human traffickers and slave masters, and wants more than anything to use us to do the work of freeing them from the bondage in which others have placed them.

Fortunately, there is much that each of us can do to help, with little or no interruption or change to our lifestyle.

Speak Up!

There is nothing the criminals involved in the modern-day atrocities of human trafficking and slavery—the recruiters, the traffickers, the pimps, and others—want more than for decent people to remain ignorant about what they do. All they ask is that we do nothing. Simple silence. If the myth that "it doesn't happen here" can prevail, they have won.

Knowing that, one of the answers to the question, "What can I do?" is to look for opportunities to talk to others about these horrible abuses against our fellow human beings. We can follow the examples of Moses and Jesus, who courageously spoke out against the injustices of their time. Follow the historic examples of John Wesley, William Wilberforce, and Harriet Tubman and other godly people who spoke out against the enslavement of fellow human beings during a time when people didn't want to hear what they had to say.

If you become aware of a situation in which human trafficking could be involved, don't just sit by and wait for someone else to speak up or act. Notify your local authorities, or call the Trafficking Information and Referral Hotline at 1-888-3737-888. This hotline, which is toll free and open twenty-four hours, is staffed by specialists who will help you determine if you have actually encountered a case of human trafficking, will identify resources available in your community to help victims, and help you coordinate with local social service organizations to help protect and serve victims so they can begin the process of restoring their lives. The website is http://www.acf.hhs.gov/trafficking/.

Your words may or may not make a huge dent in the modern-day slave trade, but they could very possibly save the life of someone's daughter or son.

Discussion Questions for Chapter 2

Truly I tell you, whatever you did for one of the least of these brothers and sisters of mine, you did for me.

—MATTHEW 25:40

1. Did Given's story of slavery happening right inside churches surprise you? How can we be as wise as serpents, yet as gentle as doves (Matthew 10:16) in matters such as this?

2. John 4:7–26 tells the story of Jesus' interaction with the woman at the well. Is there a part of that story to which you can relate? Why or why not?

3. Harriet Tubman's life was one that had an impact on lives for generations to come. Is there something in her life that inspires you to take a stand against modern-day slavery? If so, what might you do to take that stand?

4. Can you speculate about why God designed the lineage of Jesus to contain Rahab?

5. Find a recent news story in which someone took action to stop modern-day slavery and discuss it.

Chapter 3

From Farm to Factory

*Where, after all, do universal human rights begin? In small places,
close to home—so close and so small that they cannot be seen on any
maps of the world. Yet they are the world of the individual person;
the neighborhood he lives in; the school or college he attends;
the factory, farm, or office where he works.*

—ELEANOR ROOSEVELT

Modern-day slaves are all around us. We unwittingly participate in helping them remain victims through acts as simple as buying manufactured products. From cell phones to fast food to clothing, so many of the places we support with our dollars each day, week, month and year contain goods produced at least in part by individuals who have been enslaved in the name of profit.

Quyen Truong,[45] a Hawaiian resident in her early thirties, isn't ashamed to tell anyone who asks about how she lost her eye. "I tell everybody when they meet me," she says in her broken English. "I'm not ashamed. My experience—nothing to be ashamed."[46] In 1999, at age twenty-one, she had relocated from North Vietnam to American Samoa with the promise of a sewing job that paid $408 a month. She needed funds to help support her younger sister and widowed mother in Vietnam, and was hoping for a better life with more money for herself as well as her family. The video she'd been shown about the job at Daewoosa helped ease the pain of leaving them behind. She would live in spacious quarters, have access to a swimming pool and be fed three nutritious meals a day.[47] What a contrast to the poverty that surrounded her in Vietnam.[48]

The buy-in was high. Neither Quyen nor her family had the $5,000 required[49] to secure the job and pay transportation expenses, but this was a chance to improve her life. Somehow she managed to scrape together the money. When she passed the sewing and fitness tests, she was thrilled. She could now fly to American Samoa and become part of a group of three hundred Vietnamese and Chinese workers making garments for companies such as Walmart, JC Penney, Sears and Target.[50]

Her dreams dissolved the moment she entered the company's barbed wire compound and saw the grim, gray walls and the massive Samoan guards who didn't speak her language and carried sticks. She had been duped. The spacious room she had been promised turned out to be prison-like quarters, with thirty-six people stuffed into a muggy hallway with minimal ventilation and bunk beds with half-inch mattresses. The bathrooms had broken toilets. Instead of clear blue water, the swimming pool she had viewed on the video was green with slime that stunk.[51]

As in so many human trafficking situations, Quyen and the other slaves were forced to work grueling hours and fed just enough to keep them alive—in this case, minimal amounts of boiled potatoes, rice and cabbage, with no meat.[52] Back in their mother country, even if they were poor they had rice cakes, along with meat and vegetable dishes on special occasions.[53]

By late 2000, Quyen had been labeled as a troublemaker at Daewoosa for objecting to the gruesome conditions and the lack of nutrition. She knew that her outspokenness could cost her. "You can beat anyone who don't listen to you," Daewoosa owner Kil Soo Lee had told a Samoan supervisor when faced with a tough deadline on a big contract. "If anyone die, I will be responsible."[54] The workers understood all too clearly that production and the bottom line were more important than their lives. One slip up, one hint of disloyalty, could prove deadly.

Lee had built his factory, located about 2,300 miles south of Honolulu, in unincorporated American Samoa.[55] The choice was no accident. The area is well known for its poor treatment of workers and pitifully low wages.[56] Yet American Samoa is a territory of the United States, so despite its record of human rights violations, garments made there carry the *Made in America* label.[57] It doesn't matter that American citizens don't sew these garments. It doesn't matter that they're produced by skilled workers kept there by force (including sexual assault) and threats of arrest, deportation and violence.

That wasn't Lee's only hold on the women. In addition to being charged from $4,000 to $8,000 to acquire their jobs—the equivalent of eight to fifteen years' salary in Vietnam or China—the workers were required to sign contracts that contained a three-year commitment and a $5,000 penalty for breaching that agreement.[58] Many of them had sold their homes and/or borrowed money from relatives or loan sharks to follow a dream that promised stability and financial gain. They had little to return to. Just to make sure they would continue to grow the company's profits, which totaled $8 million in 1999, Lee also confiscated the workers' passports and alien registration cards.[59]

Armed security guards in a compound that more closely resembled a penal complex than a factory enforced Lee's intimidation tactics. In November of 2000, Lee ordered his guards to attack any workers who tried to defy his authority[60] or who were working too slowly.[61] As the guard came toward Quyen with a raised length of PVC pipe, the young woman knew she was in danger. The beating, which would literally and figuratively scar her for life, continued for what seemed like an eternity. She didn't think the pain could get any worse until her assailant raised the PVC pipe and poked it into her eye socket. She would lose her eye as a result.[62]

To this day, Quyen relives the experience. "It's like a movie that plays over and over, and I cannot stop it when it happens," she told the media after being rescued. "Injury to the body can be mended, but injury to the soul and mental being…what can a doctor do to treat you?"[63]

The workers were eventually rescued when one of the captives managed to toss an SOS note from the window of a company car. The note was found and passed along to the Department of Labor.[64]

The prosecution of Lee in 2003 on fourteen counts,[65] including holding workers in a condition of involuntary servitude and conspiring to violate civil rights, was at that time one of the biggest modern-day slavery case in U.S. history.[66] But it is far from the only one.

Products Made by Slave Labor?

How do we know if the shirt we just purchased as a Christmas gift—or the well-made slacks that are such a good buy—were made by a legitimate garment factory or by a place like this factory? The short answer is we usually can't be certain that a product doesn't have slave labor in its composition at some place along the line. As illustrated in the above story, just because a product is marked "Made in America" doesn't guarantee that the product is not, at least in part, a result of slave labor.

Although the stories of individuals victimized by predators like Kil Soo Lee are distressing and far too numerous, the vast majority of slave-made products come from China. The Chinese have found a way to convert some of their prison population into prison factories (called *Laojiao*), which incarcerate those the government feels are a threat to national security or considers unproductive. The practice has become lucrative business for China.

Conceptually, this may sound like a wise plan to keep the prison population busy in a constructive way that benefits their country. In China, however, a person can be arrested for disagreeing with the government or for religious practices not sanctioned by the government. Charges may be something like "not engaging in honest pursuits" or "being able-bodied but refusing to work,"[67] so those charged are not entitled to the same judicial procedures as some other offenders, and may be sent directly to prison via an administrative sentence by local public security forces. Additionally, due to Chinese governmental policies, 70 percent of prisoners are not released at the completion of their sentences but are held at the prison and must continue working there.[68]

Enslaved for Their Faith

The prison factory system of *Laojiao* has become a way to deter and eliminate opposition groups, including but not limited to those who have been a part of Christian churches that fall outside the government church. Indeed, as shocking as it may sound, our regular buying habits may mean that we're supporting the slave labor of some of our Chinese brothers and sisters imprisoned for their faith.[69]

While there are laws against importing slave-made products into the United States, the Chinese get around those laws because each *Laojiao* camp has both a camp name and a public name. The Shanghai Municipal Prison, for example, is also referred to as the Shanghai Printing and Stationery Factory. In *Human Rights Brief*, Ramin Pegan writes, "Financial information on ninety-nine forced labor camp enterprises collected by Dunn and Bradstreet was released on June 30, 1999. According to this data, the ninety-nine camps had total annual sales of U.S. $842.7 million. These camps represent only 9 percent of the roughly 1,100 known *Laojiao* camps."[70] When the factories are discovered by the outside world, the Chinese government simply closes and moves them, or reopens them under other names.

That is not to imply that all slave-made goods that are imported into the United States are from China or even that all Chinese-made goods are from *Laojiaos*, but it is another example of how slave-made goods permeate our buying habits here in America.

It's hard to tell whether goods—including lamps, toys, tote bags, clothing, kitchen gadgets, electronics and more—are the product of forced labor. The fact is that none of us would willingly purchase slave-produced merchandise. But since slavery in America's farms is among the top forms of slavery in our beloved United States, it's possible we are doing just that as we head to the market or to a restaurant for food.

Debt Bondage

Slavery in domestic agriculture—as well as in almost all other forms of human trafficking—usually takes the form of debt bondage. In this form of financial control and intimidation, the captor keeps a tab for all the victim's "expenses." These may include (but are not limited to) transportation costs for the victim to arrive to the place where he or she is operating as a modern-day slave, along with food, shelter, medical expenses, clothing, tips, and anything else needed for everyday life. For those trapped in the sex trade, expenses can also include manicures, makeup, hair styling, condoms, costumes, photo sessions, advertising, and protection. In debt bondage, in the best-case scenario, the worker's debt ends up being many times the amount that he or she originally agreed to pay to acquire the job. In the worst-case scenario, it becomes a tool captors use to keep their slaves imprisoned.

In short, the system is designed to keep slaves working harder than they've ever worked, harder than any human being should be required to work, and the slaveholder sees to it the debt always meets or exceeds the salary owed. Additionally, forcing slaves to buy in company stores with inflated markups helps ensure that victims will never be able to repay their escalating debt no matter how many hours they put in. According to evidence in the 1998 El Monte, California sweatshop case where seventy-two Thai garment workers were kept for eight years in slavery and debt bondage, the company store that the workers were obliged to use charged $20 for a simple bar of soap.[71]

In Kevin Bales' and Ron Soodalter's book *The Slave Next Door*, Lucas Benitez described the process of enslavement:

> *Debt begins when the coyote turns you over to the crew leader. So many of our compañeros have suffered in this way and say being sold...feels worse than being an animal...You get sold for $500, but the next day the debt is $1,000. Then they add on rent and food, and your debt increases.... If you have a slow day in the fields, the crew leader will say 'you owe us more now; you didn't work well.' You never see the check stubs, so you have no idea where you stand with your debt.*[72]

When victims finally become so weary of their living situation that they muster up the courage to ask their captor to set them free, they are told they must first repay the debt they have incurred. This not only keeps victims enslaved, it allows the perpetrator to demand more and greater output from the slaves. Physical and psychological abuses inflicted on the slaves help cement those demands, as does the victims' hope that they will be able to pay off the debt if they just work hard enough. Ironically, that goal often diverts their thoughts from the truth of the matter, which is that they are slaves, and cannot leave without threat of physical harm or death.

How can this be happening in our very own country? We have to, again, look at our sense of hierarchy. As a child, I remember the caution from my parents as I was helping prepare fresh fruits and vegetables for dinner. "Wash that carefully," they would tell me. "Remember, the last person to handle it was a migrant worker with dirty hands." That vision was enough for me to carefully scrub the tomato or apple, sometimes even with soap.

But who *are* these migrant workers with dirty hands? People of lesser value than those who live in our neighborhood? Possibly in the eyes of society they are. However, in reality, they are someone's mother or father, sister, brother, husband or wife, someone's child, and for those of us who believe the Bible, they are certainly a child of God. In God's eyes, those are precious children, just as we are. God sees them as no more, and no less, than any one of us.

Antonio Martinez was what some would term a migrant worker. However, a closer look at his life reveals he could be more accurately described as a slave.[73]

In Hidalgo, Mexico, Antonio was the oldest of six children. He felt the responsibility to support his family because his parents were not in good health.[74] One day he met a contractor, also known as a *coyote*, who promised him construction work in California if Antonio would pay him some 16,000 pesos or about 1,700 American dollars to get across the border into the U.S. That was a fortune to Antonio. He couldn't possibly make—let alone save—a sum like that in Mexico. The *coyote* reassured him. Paying the money back would be easy once Antonio had crossed the border and secured his construction job, he said. [75]

Two weeks later, Antonio and more than three-dozen other hopefuls boarded a bus to the land of opportunity. At the Sonora desert, the bus stopped and new *coyotes* took responsibility for the travelers. Antonio was placed in a group led by a man named Chino. For the next three days, Antonio and his group hiked across the hot, dry desert with just a single day of supplies.[76]

Finally, hungry, thirsty and exhausted, they crossed the border and were driven to a house in Tucson. Instead of being fed and given a chance to rest, Chino ordered Antonio and the others to hand over more cash. Antonio was broke. He had nothing. The ensuing threats of violence made him realize just how helpless he'd suddenly become. But there was no turning back now. He had no funds and no documentation. He was at the *coyote's* mercy.[77]

Then came what must have sounded like good news. Although Antonio wouldn't be given the promised construction job in California, he would be sent to Florida to make a $150 a day in the tomato fields.[78] That was a lot of money! His momentary sense of hope, however, proved false.

Chino turned Antonio and seventeen other Mexican workers over to a van driver called El Chacal—the jackal—who crammed them all into the back of a van and made them sit on the floor to escape the authorities' notice.[79] For four days, the van only stopped for gasoline. Even then, its passengers were not allowed to get out. As documented later in a criminal report by senior patrol agent Jose M. Lopez of the U.S. Immigration agency, "During the trip, the men in the group were made to urinate in plastic jugs, and the woman...did not urinate until two days into the trip, when the van had to stop to repair a flat tire, because she was unable to use the jug."[80] Although the migrants were given just two bags of chips to share during the entire trip to Florida, each was charged $700 to be paid in hard labor.[81]

Upon his arrival in South Florida, Antonio and the other workers who had been crammed into the back of the van were taken to a labor camp run by Abel and Basilio Cuello.[82] Any lingering expectations about improving his situation evaporated when Antonio heard El Chacal and the Cuellos haggling over his price tag. El Chacal was demanding $500 for him and each of the other migrants, and the Cuellos were offering $350 each. "We were being sold like animals," Antonio recalls.[83]

The migrants worked long hard hours in the field. The way the debt and wages were structured, however, made it virtually impossible to repay the amount supposedly owed and free themselves from the debt bondage that enslaved them.

They were housed in a mobile home at 1365 Sanctuary Road in Immolakee, Florida.[84] Despite its name, the home on Sanctuary Road was anything but a sanctuary, with mattresses on the floor and only four or five dishes to share the inadequate meals that left them hungry. "I thought I was going to die there, because I didn't eat well," Antonio recalls.[85] There were roaches everywhere and holes in the floor, exposing snakes below. One of Antonio's co-workers awoke one night with a scorpion sting on his neck.[86]

Worse than the grim conditions, Antonio and the two-dozen others that were stuffed into the small mobile home couldn't leave. The Cuellos made sure of that by locking them in at night. Abel Cuello would show up in the morning to unbolt the door and drive them to the fields.[87] This daily transportation to the fields where they were enslaved was charged against their wages, along with rent for their nightly prison, the scant amounts of food they were fed and the foul water that was supplied.[88] Workers used the little amount of salary left to purchase toiletries and food on those infrequent occasions that their captors took them to a small nearby grocery.[89]

An opportunity to escape presented itself during one of those rare outings to the store when Cuello fell asleep while standing guard outside. Despite threats of violence[90] should they try to flee, when Antonio and the others saw him napping, they seized their chance and raced to the highway and eventually to safety.[91]

"For four and a half months, I was held in forced labor in the fields against my will, and it seemed like an eternity for me," Antonio says. "They were watching me all the time, controlling all I did. I thought I was going to die. Thanks to God I was able to escape, and it allowed me to become more aware. I'm out here learning more every day."[92]

Cuello pleaded guilty to one count of involuntary servitude. In 1999, he went to prison and served thirty-three months. Two of his relatives, who were co-defendants, were also convicted.[93] Before Cuello went to prison he spotted Antonio and gave chase in his Chevy Suburban, demanding his coyote fee back and swearing at the top of his lungs.[94] According to the *Miami Herald*, Cuello has since created another harvesting company based in Naples, FL.[95]

Anti-slavery advocates believe there are many, many male and female slaves working in our fields and factories. Indeed, the numbers are so high that these slave-based operations often remain undetected. Meanwhile, the personal tragedies continue to mount.

In 1999, a young Guatemalan woman by the name of Maria Choz was forced to come to this country when native Guatemalan Jose Tecum, who owned the largest home in their community, threatened to kill Maria or her father if she wasn't given to him. Tecum then smuggled Maria into the United States.[96]

Authorities responded to a domestic call at Tecum's home in Immokalee, FL. Officers observed that Maria "cried and visibly shook."[97] She said she was required to do whatever Tecum ordered—including servicing him sexually—and that she considered herself a slave. Her labor for Tecum included work at a local farm. During the trial, the prosecutor nailed Tecum, saying, "Every paycheck she earned, he took it. And she received maybe one or two or three dollars."[98]

Maria's response in court reminds me of so many other victims. "I don't want to look at his face," she responded when prosecutors requested that she identify Tecum.[99] Fear, shame and pain often prompt such a response. Victims innately know they never deserved to be treated as subhuman beings in the first place, but sorting that out in their hearts, lives and minds is a process that takes many years and sometimes is never achieved.

Tap the Power of the Purse

Slave-produced products are all around us—from the garments, made by slaves with "Made in the USA" tags and products made by our brothers and sisters imprisoned in China for their faith, to the food that we eat every day. Other goods tarnished with the slave trade include cell phones, automobiles, jewelry, cosmetics, electronics, sports equipment, rugs, and agricultural produce including tomatoes, sugar, tea, coffee, chocolate and seafood.

If so many of the things we use in our daily lives are tainted by slavery, how can we possibly avoid every product that has slavery in its line? How do we know that the shirt we're wearing, the cell phone we're carrying or the taco with tomatoes we're eating hasn't been affected by slavery? The simple answer is we often can't. At least not yet. The vast scope of the problem makes it impossible to identify every product with slaves in its production and/or delivery, which is all the more reason to fight against slavery.

As we all become more aware and bring awareness to those around us, however, we can each help break the chain of slavery within the products we use every day. That doesn't mean boycotting an entire industry, which is often the concerned consumer's knee-jerk reaction. Just as not all goods coming from China are made by slaves, not all of any type of product is slave made. In fact, even in those products such as chocolate or diamonds or tomatoes known to be contaminated by slavery, only a small percentage of that product has slave labor in its production and delivery. So if we boycott the purchase of all chocolate, diamonds or tomatoes, we hurt the vast majority of those supplying slavery-free products in return for a fair profit.

A 2010 documentary entitled *The Dark Side of Chocolate* tells the secrets behind child slavery in the Ivory Coast. Children between the ages of eleven and fifteen are coerced or kidnapped from their homes. The men who worked undercover to make the documentary filmed one man telling plantation owners that he could supply them with children for labor for about two hundred thirty Euros each (that was his price before the typical bargaining ensued). Included in the price was transport and delivery of the children to their buyer, who would have the use indefinitely of each child for whatever purposes they chose.

Traffickers are motivated by money. By cutting off their income stream, we can stop slavery at its root. We can affect their profits by requesting fair trade items and informing those around us about the need for fair trade. Tragedies like the kidnapping and enslavement of children on the Ivory Coast will only be averted by taking away the demand and profitability.

So what can you and I do as consumers? We can insist on fair trade products. Purchasing fair trade products is one of the best and safest ways to assure that whatever we are purchasing is not tainted with slavery. After being informed by that documentary, I have pledged to buy only fair trade chocolate products. I can't in good conscience eat chocolate when, in my mind, I see enslaved children. While my efforts don't in and of themselves solve the problem, I know each small piece and each single consumer in the puzzle is important.

A unique business model for fair trade products brings together producers and buyers with the common goal of creating a sustainable living wage for those involved with the products' production. Buyers and producers work in cooperation, adhering to a set of fair trade criteria established by the International Fair Trade Association for handicrafts or the Fair Trade Labeling Organization for agricultural commodities. The criteria include fair wages, good working conditions, safety procedures and adequate health standards for all workers. Producers also agree to adhere to environmentally-sound production methods. Finally, buyers and producers also must promote human rights, especially the rights of the disenfranchised—women, children and those with disabilities.[100]

When the opportunity arises, buying fair trade items ensures that the product was not produced with slave labor. But fair trade products aren't always available. That's where you can make an active difference. Take time to go to the store manager and ask about a product. Politely state that fair trade items that do not contain slavery in their production line are important to you and ask the manager to make the appropriate calls to ensure that no slavery taints the product. He or she may or may not be able to actually give you the information you need. Even so, you'll have alerted the manager to the fact that selling free trade items, as well as items without slavery in their production, is important to a sector of their clients. That will influence their future buying decisions. And we all know how loudly money talks.

With the advancements of technology and the determination and innovation of some great abolitionists, buying slave-free products is about to get easier. Check a website called free2work.org and you may find some items you are contemplating purchasing, or items you already own. This site lists many products, manufacturers and suppliers, and gives each a letter grade from A to F based on forty standards. The researchers who publish their information on the site, for example, monitor where a tire manufacturer is getting the rubber for its tire and conduct spontaneous spot checks to ensure that the supply chain remains clean of slavery. They also note whether individual brands have a policy about labor conditions and comment on the transparency of their supply chain.

"We assume most people don't want to wear other people's tragedy, and that they don't want to tread on other people's dreams with their shoes," says Not For Sale president and co-founder David Batstone.[101] "Our goal is that you can walk into a Target or a Safeway and find a grade on most of the products in that store." In keeping with that objective, he is working with brilliant, innovative minds to develop technology such as applications for smart phones. With these smart phones, you'll be able to take a photo of a bar code and the grade for that product will appear, enabling you to make the conscious choice to buy products whose companies are intentionally eliminating slavery in the supply chain. This kind of monetary pressure will result in a demand shift by consumers that will reduce and eventually eliminate slave-tainted products.[102]

Some of the world's brightest individuals have joined in the fight against slavery so stay tuned to this movement. Outside-of-the-box ideas like these will help us end modern-day slavery, as long as you, the consumer, choose to support them.

Discussion Questions for Chapter 3

*Love the Lord your God with all your heart and with all your soul
and with all your strength and with all your mind
and Love your neighbor as yourself.*

—Luke 10:27

1. Is it surprising to you that an item labeled "Made in America" could have slave labor in its chain of manufacturing or delivery? How might one ensure that they are not purchasing slave-made products?

2. Explain how the *Laojiao* system works in China. If we purchase products from a *Laojiao* how might we actually be supporting the persecution of Christians?

3. What is debt bondage? How does it assist traffickers in keeping their victims enslaved?

4. Not all migrant workers are slaves. What is the difference between a migrant worker who is a slave and one who is simply working crops for a fair wage?

5. How can boycotting a particular product, such as cocoa, harm those who are not involved with human trafficking?

6. Find a labor trafficking case in the news and discuss it.

Chapter 4

Just the Help

Slavery is one of those monsters of darkness
to whom the light of truth is death.

—FREDERICK DOUGLASS

Slavery is clearly woven into each of our lives. It doesn't just lie hidden on farms and in factories. In too many cases, you don't have to look any further than your own neighborhood—yes, your own backyard—to find modern-day slaves.

Tina Font didn't react when she began to spot the same slender, dark-haired young girl in her neighbor's house doing dishes night after night at 10 p.m., 11 p.m. and even as late as midnight. "We didn't put two and two together," the Irvine, California resident says.[103] Neighbors like Font had no way of knowing that little thirteen-year-old Shyima Hall had already spent three years being forced to work up to twenty hours a day for the Egyptian couple who had purchased her from her parents a year before coming to the United States.[104]

While other children were at school, Shyima, who stood not much taller than the countertop where she did the dishes, was forced to do the family's wash and the ironing, get the children (including one girl her own age) ready for school, cook their food, and clean the inside and outside of their lavish Tuscan-style home, including mopping the marble floors and dusting the crystal chandeliers.

Instead of joining the family for meals, Shyima ate alone. At every turn, she was made to feel that she was less than the other family members. "They called me stupid girl," she recalls.[105] That's when they called her anything at all.

After grueling work days that sometimes lasted up to twenty hours, the tiny girl would finally collapse on a filthy, bare mattress in the windowless garage, which was neither air-conditioned nor heated. She lived there in darkness, since the only light bulb had burned out shortly after her arrival and was never replaced. Shyima's captors even demanded that she do her own laundry in a bucket by her mattress, saying that her clothes were too dirty for the washing machine.[106]

Still, Shyima never considered running away. "I thought this was normal," she says.[107] She would scarcely have had the chance even if she had wanted to flee, since she was never allowed outside the family house unaccompanied. Besides, she had been repeatedly told that if she told anyone about her situation, the police would come and take her away because she was in the country illegally.[108]

Finally, someone did notice that something wasn't right. On April 9, 2002, an anonymous call, probably from a neighbor, alerted authorities that a young girl who seemed to be a maid rather than a member of the family was living in the garage and not attending school. When an Orange County Child Protective Services social worker responded, the sight of Shyima's shabby brown T-shirt, baggy pants and raw, red hands told her what she needed to know. When Shyima, through a translator, confirmed that she hadn't attended school during the two years she'd been in the U.S., she was taken into protective custody, and the husband and wife who had enslaved her were arrested and charged with involuntary servitude, obtaining the labor of another person illegally, conspiracy and harboring an alien.[109]

During their 2006 trial, the couple argued that Shyima had been a member of the family. She even accompanied us on a trip to Disneyland, they told the court. They neglected to add that she had been there only to carry the family's bags, and had not been allowed to go on any rides.[110] Shyima broke down. "Where was their loving when it came to me?" she told the court, unable to hold back her sobs. "Wasn't I a human being, too? I felt like I was nothing when I was with them."[111]

After years of therapy and three foster homes, Shyima, now in her early twenties, has finally found a family, a life, a cause and a dream. She's determined to become a U.S. Immigration and Customs Enforcement (ICE) agent like Mark Abend, the ICE supervisory special agent who headed up the investigation that led to her captors' conviction. In the meantime, she speaks publicly about her plight and the need for people to keep their eyes open, stressing that human trafficking happens in even the most affluent communities. "Take your chances," she told one group gathered to hear about her experience and learn how to prevent human trafficking. "You might just save somebody's life."[112]

Sold—or Hoodwinked—Into Slavery

Shyima is one of the 14,500 to 17,500 people[113] trafficked into the U.S. every year. In Egypt, as in many African countries, it is a common—albeit illegal—practice for destitute families to sell their children in order to make ends meet.

Although some human trafficking victims like Shyima are sold into slavery or kidnapped, the majority are tricked into going with their trafficker. They think they will be doing something different than the life of slavery in which they become trapped. Non-U.S. victims are often told that they will be provided with a visa and a job, which will allow them to send funds back to their impoverished family staying behind. Once the victim has been duped or coerced into coming to this country with the trafficker, promises are broken and the game is changed. And what the victim may have thought was the opportunity of a lifetime becomes a nightmare.

When Charito*,[114] a stunningly beautiful thirty-two-year-old master chef working in a five-star hotel in Manila, read in the classifieds that an American-based Asian restaurant was looking for kitchen staff, she figured that the opportunity would be a good career move. The hotel had treated her very well, providing yearly bonuses as well as benefits. She loved her work and enjoyed those with whom she worked. She also loved her family—including her police officer father, stay-at-home mother and two brothers—with whom she lived. She would miss them all. But relocating to the U.S. would move her even higher up the career ladder and provide a better lifestyle as well.

Charito had heard of the land of plenty in America. This was exactly the next step she needed. She would get to travel, learn new things, meet new people and she would earn enough money to visit her family in the Philippines regularly. She had no reason to believe that she wouldn't be treated fairly. She had always treated others fairly and found people usually treated her well in return.

The restaurant interviewed fifty applicants and offered positions to just two—Charito and one other woman. Charito's tremendous excitement about being picked, however, was tempered by having to say goodbye to her family. She knew with her dad's poor health, her parents would never be able to visit her. It would be up to her to get back to the Philippines to see them.

When her plane landed in the U.S., people from the restaurant met her as she came out of customs. As they shuffled her and the other young woman into the van, she was in awe of the American cities and the countryside they passed during the three hours to her new home.

The very next day, she was presented with a contract that would bind her to her new employer for several years, with large penalties if she broke the contract. She had no option. She had to sign.

As soon as she began work, she knew something wasn't right. Her gruff and demanding new boss was impossible to please no matter how hard she worked. The first day was as long as the work was difficult. Charito started at 9 a.m. before the restaurant opened. Hours of chopping vegetables, chicken and other meat was hard work. When it came time for her lunch break, she was allowed to eat only the fat and skin trimmed off the chicken and the stems of the mushrooms and spinach and other waste. Between the jetlag from the trip, the long hours and the lack of food, she quickly became absolutely exhausted. But she continued to work for an hour after the restaurant closed at 10 p.m. Then, after fourteen unrelenting hours, she was told that she had not finished her work and would have to pack up some of the carrots and make them into little flowers while she was home that evening.

The next day was much the same, except that Charito, whose nature had always been loving and friendly, was reprimanded for talking with her co-workers. Charito had always quietly sung while she cooked and worked in the kitchen, but management forbade that, too, along with any other noises deemed unnecessary for the work. Even laughing was prohibited. Her boss also advised her that there would be stiff penalties if she were caught talking to Americans, whether at the restaurant, on her way home, or wherever else she happened to be.

Physical, Mental and Emotional Damage

Only after Charito had worked for a full week was she finally was given a day off. She moved into a very small apartment that she shared with a co-worker. They weren't there much.

The restaurant was staffed by Americans and Mexicans who were paid by the hour, and Asian individuals on salary. Naturally, the bulk of the work went to the latter. So Charito and her compatriots were required to labor however many hours it took to complete their tasks, which seemingly never ended. They worked in the restaurant six days a week, anywhere from twelve to fifteen hours a day. And just as she had the first day, Charito had to take home unfinished tasks as well.

Working in such a demanding and rigid environment would have been bad enough, but she was also subjected to emotional abuse. Fear, the restaurant management believed, would prompt their workers to perform better. Charito was regularly yelled at and told that she was stupid and ugly. When she wasn't being berated for nearly everything she did, Charito, along with the other Asian workers, was the brunt of nasty jokes, which proved particularly humiliating.

"People look at me like I steal money or something," she recalled. "I was so embarrassed."

When Charito's manager noticed a customer's concern during one such tirade, she cradled Charito's chin like a caring, loving friend and said, "I just care so much about you and I worry for you because you're a liar, you shouldn't do things like that, you're a liar." The demeaning words further damaged Charito, especially since they led the customer to believe that she was a lying and ungrateful employee.

The emotional trauma would erase childhood memories—from favorite songs to the name of her first school—from her mind. When she finally began to remember those details a couple of years after escaping the job, she felt like she was finally returning to life. She was luckier than another Asian worker at the restaurant, who according to Charito "completely lost his mind" due to the harsh psychological treatment. "He walk around like a tree, walked around everywhere and say nothing to anyone."

The disrespect Charito had to contend with didn't just come from the owners and the managers. The Mexican male workers would touch her bottom as they walked by. When she called them on it, they always told her it was an accident, but she knew better. All the Asian women who worked at the restaurant were being groped. When she complained to the owner she was told, "You know you're not a beauty queen, you're not Miss USA, you're not a famous model. Why would they want to touch your bottom? You know you're not a star, they wouldn't even want to touch you." It became obvious that the men were allowed to cop their feels, and neither she nor the other Asian women working there had any recourse.

The stress and grueling schedule quickly began to wear on her. After just a few months, Charito would look in the mirror when she got home and say to herself that she looked ten years older than she had when she left the Philippines. Shortly thereafter, she began to lose her hair. Thankfully, the kitchen hat she was required to wear at work spared her the embarrassment of being seen in that condition. Her hands would go next, victims of carpal tunnel syndrome that stemmed from the daily long strenuous hours of repetitive motions.

Charito was not used to being mistreated, so she complained. "Party's over. Go home," the manager told her. "But first pay me six thousand dollars; you signed a contract." He added that the restaurant had control over her work visa. "In a dispute, the government will believe us, not you, because we're a big and powerful American restaurant." Charito felt she had nowhere to turn.

The Price of Defiance

A short time later the owner, who Charito had originally approached with her grievances, wandered back to the kitchen where Charito was slaving away. As he casually walked by her, he said, "If you go back to the Philippines and I see you on the sidewalk, you might want to be careful. An accident could happen to you." The threat was clear and only slightly veiled. Charito's life was in danger unless she complied with all her employer was requiring of her.

After two years, someone finally reported the restaurant to the Labor Bureau. Agency investigators eventually determined that the Asian people were being under-compensated and that the number of hours they were working was far beyond what was allowed by law.

"Did things get better then?" I asked Charito when I interviewed her.

"No. Then we had to punch in. We worked forty hours a week, plus ten hours overtime and we punched out. But we were forced to work just as many hours as before and still had to take work home and were not paid for any of it."

To make matters worse, in addition to working the same long hours and continuing to take additional work home, the restaurant *cut* Charito's pay by about 25 percent.

Finally, she had taken all she thought she could possibly endure. After another public humiliation, numb from the painful exhaustion permeating her body and her now severely injured hands and arms, Charito walked out the door.

"I walked home for several blocks in the rain," she says. When she got back to her apartment, she didn't even have the strength or motivation to change into dry clothes. "I sat in the corner of the room in my apartment curled up in a ball, and cried and cried until I fell asleep." The sleep didn't last long. All too soon, she heard people sent by her manager calling for her outside her window. She didn't feel like talking to anyone, and she knew whatever they said would not be pleasant. She couldn't take any more of their demoralizing and carefully crafted degradation, so she remained curled up in the corner of her apartment. In response, she heard her window break as a rock sailed through and landed on the floor. She understood her employer's wordless message. "We are watching you," he was saying. "You won't get away with this."

"I was so afraid, I didn't want to touch the curtain," says Charito. "I was too scared to move. I was cold and all my body shake, and they call, call, call, call. I'm crying and I'm sleeping, I sleep in the corner, all my body wet and dirty. And I kept thinking, 'This is not right, this is America, this is not right.'"

The next day she got up, showered and went to work. One look at her manager, and she bolted. The manager grabbed her and physically restrained her. "I couldn't talk, like there was something stuck in my throat and I cry," says Charito. "I want to run and lots of people looked at me." Charito tried to get away, but the manager took her by the waist and pulled her closer, saying, "Oh, I was so worried about you. You shouldn't do things like that, you'll hurt yourself. You need to quit lying."

That terrifying experience was typical of the abusive humiliation inflicted on Charito by her manager, and added to her chronic exhaustion and high stress. Meanwhile, Charito's carpal tunnel syndrome worsened. She now could no longer grip a knife for more than five minutes at a time. One of the servers encouraged her to see a doctor, who immediately recognized the seriousness of her physical condition. His note to Charito's employers stressed that her duties had to be changed. So they put her to work in the storeroom.

"I am 5'1" and weigh 110 pounds. I was required to haul in fifty-pound bags of rice," she recalled. "The restaurant sometimes makes over a hundred thousand dollars in one weekend. Think how much rice we served and how many rice bags must be carried." When others tried to help her lift the heavy bags, the management told them not to provide assistance, that she had to do the work by herself. "This was my punishment for going to the doctor for my hands and arms."

Getting Help

Four years after Charito had been brought to the U.S. under false pretenses, the web that her employers had woven to trap her finally began to unravel. The kind server who had insisted that Charito get medical attention for her hands and arms introduced her to a retired Philippine/American police officer who became a friend. On his birthday, Charito phoned him to wish him a happy birthday. When he heard the click, click, click in the background, he asked her about the noise.

"Oh, I'm carving carrots for work while I'm on the phone."

He asked her if they were paying her additional salary for this extra work.

"No, I do this all the time. It's part of my work. If I don't complete my work at the restaurant I must bring it home."

The ex-police officer began to ask more questions and quickly figured out that things were not right. He called a member of the state's Human Trafficking Task Force, who in turn connected Charito with a contracted government agency that helps trafficking victims navigate their way to safety, as well as with an attorney who would finally be able to stand up to her employer and claim the rights she had coming to her. As soon as her employers got wind of her actions, Charito was fired.

Today, a couple of years later, Charito is once again happy. She has had several surgeries to repair the damage to her hands and arms and still has more surgeries to come. She has moved to a new city and now works for a different restaurant. "My boss, he is so nice and so good. He says 'Thank you' to me for my hard work. He pays us fairly and even sometimes brings the staff corn dogs we can eat." She marvels at having her life back. "Before I made so little, I have no life, no car, I was going numb. I couldn't remember things—my first dog, my first car, nothing. Now I have everything I want. I have good job, they treat me and all their employees fairly and I have a car, I have lots and lots of very good friends, my life is very, very good." She has even saved enough money to return home to her family for a visit. She'll go as soon as her paperwork comes through, so she can make the trip and return, abiding by the laws of the United States, where she is pleased to live. Her family still doesn't know what happened to her. She doesn't want them to worry about her.

It is obvious this woman wasn't looking for a handout or a free ride, but really just wanted the fair salary she had been promised for a fair day's work. Her employers were investigated, but not tried for human trafficking. Due to technicalities, the charges never stuck.

As I listened to Charito during our interview, I didn't hear an ounce of resentment toward the restaurant owners and employees who had abused her so terribly. I didn't hear a bit of built-up anger or hope for vengeance. Instead, she stuck strongly to her statements of injustice and hope that everyone be treated fairly and appreciated. I thought to myself, "I could learn from her. She is a strong yet gentle woman."

I asked her what I could have done to help her if I had been a customer patronizing the restaurant where she was enslaved. "Don't complain about the food," she said. Whenever that happened, the manager came back to her area, threw the food at her and berated her unmercifully.

I said, "But what if I wanted to do more for you than that? How would I know if you were being trafficked?" She said that someone hearing the manager yelling at her and berating her might have called the National Human Trafficking Hotline (1-888-3737-888) or the head of the state Human Trafficking Task Force that eventually helped her. While one report of a worker being yelled at won't necessarily trigger an investigation, repeated reports of seeming abuse must be investigated and may result in obtaining the help the worker needs before it is too late.

Importing Slaves to the U.S.

What happened to Charito is all too common. Convincing foreign nationals to come to the United States where they'll make enough money to better their own lives, and even become able to send cash back to the families they're leaving behind, is so easy that unscrupulous individuals have turned it into big business. Thousands of people who trade their homeland for a better life for themselves and their families are funneled into employment agencies and hired out to major hotel chains, country clubs, resorts and businesses to fill housekeeping, kitchen, landscaping, janitorial, maintenance and roofing jobs, or any other duties that can be contracted out.

The sales pitch to the company sounds as appealing as the pitch to the foreign national. It goes something like this: *We can bring in laborers for your company at less expense to you than if you hire them yourself. We do the hiring, firing, cover liability and other insurances, and look after any problems. Our employees work hard and their oversight is our problem, not yours. You save money not only on salaries but also on labor disputes, liabilities, and supervisory staff.*

That's a good deal for the hiring entity, but a disaster for the laborers. For starters, they're housed in generally small, overcrowded facilities with little to no furniture. They're lucky to get an old mattress. Otherwise they sleep on the bare floor. Generally, each worker in the mixed gender units is charged about half the total rent, and with several workers in each unit that amounts to a hefty profit for the criminal enterprise that hired them. The agency oversees all the workers' mail, assuring that documents are filled out in ways that are beneficial to the agency. All other communication is restricted as well. Because the laborers come into the country on work visas that then expire, those who try to secure alternative housing are quickly intimidated by assertions that their immigrant status will be revoked and that authorities will then bring legal consequences against them.

To further tighten their hold on their labor pool, agencies keep the workers in debt bondage, which we read about in Chapter Three. The laborers are paid much less than what was promised, and the expenses the agency holds over their heads always add up to more than the workers could ever earn. Workers, however, are not allowed to seek other employment without paying the agency large sums of cash to buy out their contracts. So purchasing a plane ticket home or paying for their own living expenses while living in the U.S. becomes a financial impossibility. They're stuck.

Threats of physical harm against these foreign nationals, as well as against their friends and family both in the U.S. and in their home country, further ensure cooperation, however involuntary. Randomly carrying out such a threat when someone doesn't comply with agency mandates is another amazingly effective tool for keeping the laborers under the traffickers' control.

Recent large indictments against several employee-contracting agencies have helped spotlight these criminal operations. One indictment stated that the agency had failed to provide a proper salary or overtime pay, and failed to pay the workers in a manner set forth in the terms.[115] The company disregarded employment regulations and laws, and defrauded insurance companies in order to obtain the required insurance coverage for their employed foreign nationals illegally working in the U.S. It's a small wonder that any agency with so few scruples would likewise disrespect U.S. employment laws.

Still, too many of us remain unaware of these illegal agency operations.

That, however, was certainly not true of Maria Alvarez*, the lively house-keeper who came in to clean my Denver hotel room during a recent trip.[116] After making small talk designed to ascertain whether she was safe and working under acceptable conditions, I asked if she worked directly for the hotel or for an agency. She announced with pride and conviction that she works only directly for the hotel. She went on to tell of others she knew who had been scammed by agencies. "I'm smarter than that," she said. She had learned what to look out for after friends and relatives had been duped.

Maria knew so much more than most of us who aren't aware of the problem and don't even realize that we may come into regular contact with people who have been trafficked. As I began meeting domestic slaves through my work with victims, I would take them to places like groceries or restaurants, only to find out that they had been in those exact locations with their slaveholders. As a result, I have come to realize that when doing our daily errands, we all could be standing in line next to a slave who we don't even notice because he or she is either quiet, shy, of a different culture, or speaks little to no English. So I have learned to keep an eye out and think past the language barrier or self-protective postures when I suspect I am encountering a house slave. Most likely, the person in forced servitude doesn't even know that the people who keep her imprisoned in this job are not employers, but slaveholders and human traffickers—a.k.a. criminals—and that she is a victim of modern-day slavery.

Conned, Intimidated, Coerced

The human trafficking dynamic parallels that of domestic violence. First the perpetrator begins wooing the victim—and there's no one more charming than a person who plans to ultimately try to control his or her victim through physical and emotional abuse. Even those perpetrators who aren't particularly charming don't initiate the discussion by overtly saying, "Hey, I'm going to beat the pucky out of you if you don't do what I want." A domestic violence perpetrator comes to you and says in essence, "You are the most beautiful thing I have ever seen and I really need you, I want to be a part of your life, I'd die if I couldn't have you. We can build a beautiful life together." Likewise, the trafficker woos the victim with flattery, promises, and hopes for the future.

Whether trafficking victims are duped, intimidated or forced into slavery to function as servants, laborers or prostituted people, they suffer similar circumstances: they're over-worked, underpaid, deprived of food and medical attention, sometimes raped and often beaten.

What the victim gets and doesn't get hinges on the needs of the trafficker. Slaves are often provided with the cheapest possible food to eat that may even be rancid, and only enough of that to keep them alive so they can continue to work. There's no compassion. Decisions about how to treat slaves revolve around the trafficker's needs rather than the slaves'. If it's to the slaveholder's advantage for the person in forced servitude not to have decent clothing to go out in public, then the victim will be shoddily dressed. If that slaveholder is served by having somebody who is going to blend in, then the victim will wear nice apparel, but those clothes will usually be charged against the trafficking victim's wages at a rate much higher than the actual price paid. This prevalent tactic of debt bondage works to keep all kinds of trafficking victims enslaved.

Though it is often U.S. citizens who wind up in sex-trafficking in America, other types of modern-day slaves come from other cultures. Their language barrier compounds their deprivation and isolation. This verbal obstacle makes asking for help especially difficult once they realize their forced servitude is unjust.

Additionally, a seemingly inescapable sense of hierarchy and preconceptions prevent us from recognizing that a problem exists. Instead of focusing on the human in front of us, we see their differences. They're just the help. So we look right past them and never notice the person or the crime of trafficking that's often taking place in plain sight.

Still, some people do see what the rest of us don't. An estimated one third of the small number of slaves freed in the U.S. each year are delivered from forced servitude because someone just like you or me noticed something that didn't look right and reported it instead of walking away.[117]

That's not nearly enough. "The combination of high profits and low risk makes trafficking the fastest-growing criminal industry in the world, now second in size only to drugs with a global annual market of about $42.5 billion, according to the Council of Europe, Europe's leading human rights watchdog," writes Amy Dempsey in a Cal State Fullerton student magazine article titled "Suburban Slavery."[118] And as we've seen, it takes a pittance to keep a slave alive. "The industry requires low start-up capital and few skills to generate profits," Dempsey adds. "In many cases, a trafficker must simply be willing to exploit a vulnerable person and tap the tremendous demand that exists for cheap labor and commercial sex."[119]

The trafficker counts on us not seeing, and if we notice something unusual, minding our own business and not reporting it. Let's not empower the trafficker. When we see something that could be human trafficking, let's report it to 1-888-3737-888.

Learn to Recognize the Stench of Human Trafficking

Anyone—no matter who they are or where they live—can fall victim to human trafficking. Take time to become educated on the subject, so you'll know it when you see it. Watch a movie about human trafficking or modern-day slavery. One such movie, *Human Trafficking* starring Mira Sorvino and Donald Sutherland, was key in my decision to write this book. Spend fifteen minutes researching modern-day slavery online. Reading this book is a good step toward beginning to understand this atrocity.

Learn how to spot the signs of human trafficking. Read publications or other books on the subject, or subscribe to a newsletter of an organization that combats human trafficking.

The Polaris Project gives the information below to help to identify trafficking victims.[120] If you see any of these red flags, call the National

Human Trafficking Resource Center hotline at 1-888-3737-888 to report the situation.

Red Flags and Potential Indicators of Human Trafficking

Are you or someone you know being trafficked? Is trafficking happening in your community? Is the situation you encountered human trafficking? The following is a list of potential red flags and indicators of human trafficking.

If you see any of these red flags, call the National Human Trafficking Resource Center hotline at 1-888-3737-888 now to report the situation.

Common Work and Living Conditions
The Individual(s) in Question:

- Is not free to leave or come and go as he/she wishes
- Is under 18 and is providing commercial sex acts
- Is in the commercial sex industry and has a pimp/manager
- Is unpaid, paid very little, or paid only through tips
- Works excessively long and/or unusual hours
- Is not allowed breaks or suffers under unusual restrictions at work
- Owes a large debt and is unable to pay it off
- Was recruited through false promises concerning the nature and conditions of his/her work
- High security measures exist in the work and/or living locations (e.g. opaque windows, boarded up windows, bars on windows, barbed wire, security cameras, etc.)

Poor Mental Health or Abnormal Behavior

- Is fearful, anxious, depressed, submissive, tense, or nervous/paranoid behavior

- Exhibits unusually fearful or anxious behavior after bringing up "law enforcement"
- Avoids eye contact

Poor Physical Health

- Lacks health care
- Appears malnourished
- Shows signs of physical and/or sexual abuse, physical restraint, confinement, or torture

Lack of Control

- Has few or no personal possessions
- Is not in control of his/her own money, no financial records, or bank account
- Is not in control of his/her own identification documents (ID or passport)
- Is not allowed or able to speak for themselves (a third party may insist on being present and/or translating)

Other

- Claims of "just visiting" and inability to clarify where he/she is staying/address
- Lack of knowledge of whereabouts and/or do not know what city he/she is in
- Loss of sense of time
- Has numerous inconsistencies in his/her story

Note: This list is not exhaustive and rather represents a selection of possible indicators. Also, the red flags in this list may not be present in all trafficking cases and are not cumulative.

When and if you do ask questions to determine if someone may be trafficked, remember to be "as shrewd as snakes and as innocent as doves."[121] If you converse with someone you suspect is a victim, do it with great discretion and sensitivity, and only if he or she is alone, because asking questions in the presence of a trafficker could endanger both the victim's life and yours. Keep in mind, however, that a person truly being held in a trafficking situation will likely be unable or unwilling to answer your questions directly or at all due to fear because of the treatment or trauma he or she has endured while enslaved. That fear could also stem from threats of retribution against him or her or against friends or family, as well as from despair over a perceived sense that nothing will ever change.

The Salvation Army[122] offers the following questions to help identify trafficking victims. You may not actually be able to ask a suspected victim these questions directly, but the information will help determine whether you're dealing with a trafficking victim:

- Are you now being (or have you at one time been) held against your will?
- Were you ever forced or intimidated to do something against your will?
- Do you have a choice of where you work and how much you work?
- Have you been abused or beaten by your employers?
- Can you come and go as you please?
- Are you paid?
- How many hours/day and days/week do you work?
- Have you or your family been threatened to prevent you from leaving?
- Upon arrival in the U.S. did someone ask you to pay back a debt?
- Are you doing what you were told you would be doing in the U.S.?
- Who has your passport/identification papers?

Please note: It is important to talk to potential victims in a safe and confidential environment. If someone accompanies the victim, discretely attempt to separate the person from the individual accompanying him or her, since this person could be the trafficker.

Do not collect more information than you need. Mental health professionals, law enforcement professionals or legal experts, should be the ones conducting in-depth interviews with the potential victim.[123] Unnecessary or inappropriate questions can re-victimize the client and cause unintentional trauma.

Discussion Questions for Chapter 4

The Israelites groaned in their slavery and cried out,
and their cry for help because of their slavery went up to God.
—EXODUS 2:23

1. Why is it not necessarily better for a person to leave his or her impoverished life in another country to come and work as domestic help in the United States?

2. What might be some of the red flags that would indicate a worker is not being treated fairly and, in fact, could be a victim of human trafficking?

3. Why is it often not a good idea to ask a person one suspects of being a human trafficking victim if he or she needs help?

4. What kind of fraud can take place to trick a foreign national into moving to the United States, where he or she may become a human trafficking victim?

5. Find a news story featuring a foreign national trafficked into the United States and discuss the story.

Chapter 5

An Illusion of Pleasure

Simultaneously, in a culture that takes pride in
women's rights and professional achievements,
females are commonly portrayed as sexual commodities.
—DEMAND REPORT, SHARED HOPE INTERNATIONAL[124]

Some anti-slavery proponents believe that sex trafficking is responsible for more slaves than all other types of human trafficking combined. "Sex trafficking is a modern-day form of slavery in which a commercial sex act is induced by force, fraud, or coercion, or in which the person induced to perform such an act is under the age of eighteen years," explains a fact sheet published by the Administration for Children and Families division of the U.S. Department of Health and Human Services.[125] "As defined by the TVPA [Trafficking Victims Protection Act], the term 'commercial sex act' means any sex act on account of which anything of value is given to or received by any person."[126]

Appallingly, sex trafficking has reached pandemic levels worldwide, with victims forced into various forms of commercial sexual exploitation including pornography, stripping, live-sex shows, prostitution and mail-order brides.[127] To meet this growing demand, criminal traffickers deceive, coerce, and kidnap unthinkable numbers of women and children, whom they funnel into sex trafficking. Indeed, findings reported in the U.S. House of Representatives' "End Demand for Sex Trafficking Act of 2005" reveal that 100,000 to 300,000 U.S. children under eighteen are at risk for commercial sexual exploitation every year.[128] And that doesn't even count the thousands of young women eighteen and over who are trafficked into lives of degradation and pain.

The pornography business preys on these unsuspecting, vulnerable women and youngsters, as well as some young men, in order to satisfy the cravings of their mostly male customers. These johns try to convince themselves that they're committing a victimless crime—if they even consider it a crime at all—and that willing participants are receiving pleasure. They're wrong on two counts. Many of the people on film are not there voluntarily. And most are treated like the slaves they are, as the story of Haley* and her mother, Renee*, clearly reveals.[129]

Slaves Not Models

Haley's voice was more excited than Renee had ever heard it on the phone. "They like me! No more working retail for me, Mom! I'm going to be a model!" Just the tone of Haley's voice made Renee happy, too. Haley had struggled since her graduation from high school two years ago to get money for college tuition and books. She wondered what kind of college classes she could take to prepare her for the modeling career to which she really aspired.

Renee, as all parents, wanted the very best for her daughter. Together they had carefully checked the modeling agency ads, weeding out the ones that looked even the slightest bit shady.

"I go back tomorrow at 2 p.m.; they want me to sign a contract! They said they have a client who is nationally known and I'm exactly what the client is looking for. Oh Mom, I can't believe this is happening to me!

They're going to fly me to Los Angeles right away to begin training, and I'll be making anywhere from five thousand dollars to twenty thousand dollars a month! Are you happy for me?"

Renee *was* happy for her daughter. Even so, she had some concerns. She worried that Haley would become thin and unhealthy. And even though she and Haley had carefully checked out the recognized agency, she realized that there would be no accounting for unscrupulous employees who did not share the upstanding principles the agency advertised.

Still, the last thing she wanted was to squelch Haley's joy. Renee knew that Haley had always wanted to be a star. As early as kindergarten, she had longed for a microphone so she could sing and dance. By her early teens, it was evident to all that Haley was a beauty from head to toe. She had done a couple of small modeling jobs and loved the camera. Even so, she never seemed to be able to get her big break. Now, finally, someone had seen the talent and beauty that had been Haley's trademark her whole life. Not only could she finally become all she wanted to be, she would be paid great money. And that would help more than Renee even wanted to admit.

Renee had raised Haley by herself since her daughter was just four, after Haley's dad left them. With no outside help financially or otherwise, she and Haley had managed to muddle through, becoming in the process an inseparable team who were as close as mother and daughter could be.

Although for years Renee made good money as a manager in a large software firm, she had lost her job eight months prior due to the recession. To get by, mother and daughter had sold many of their belongings. The house, car, and many of their valuable possessions were gone. In the minimized world with which they had become acquainted, tuition and paying for Haley's college expenses were out of the scope of necessities. So the job offered to Haley appeared to be a godsend.

That night, Renee prepared Haley's favorite chicken cacciatore dinner, and the two laughed and dreamed about how life would be when Haley made it to the big time. Haley tried to describe everyone she'd met at the agency, happily adding that she'd already spotted some gorgeous male models.

As Renee tried to sleep that night, the darkness seemed to bring with it all the worries that can haunt a mother. The next morning as they were bustling around their rental apartment, she asked Haley if it would be okay for her to stop in at the agency. She wanted to meet all the new folks Haley was dealing with for herself.

"Mom! I'm an adult, I'm fine!" Haley exclaimed. "But I would like you to meet everyone; you're going to love them. Why don't you stop in about 4:30? We should be finished with the paperwork by then."

Renee couldn't wait for the end of the day. Everything about the agency had checked out, but this was her baby. Well, not baby anymore, but her only child. She would die before she would let anything happen to her.

Sometimes Skepticism Isn't Enough

Renee walked in the door of the agency at 4:30 p.m. sharp. The friendly receptionist seemed to be expecting her and after a warm welcome, brought her to one of the back offices where Haley sat with two staff members. As Renee walked in, the agency employees quickly looked at each other before giving her a warm welcome. "I can see where Haley gets her looks. The fruit didn't fall far from the tree! Which one is the mother and which one is the daughter?!" All four laughed. As young looking and gorgeous as Renee was, the question was ridiculous.

The staff members quickly recapped how excited they were to have found and signed Haley, and then began talking to Renee about joining the agency as well. The money they promised after initial training had been completed was unbelievable. Drawing on her financial background, Renee asked some key questions to verify the legitimacy of the offer and the operation. The answers all seemed believable.

A quick photo shoot to see how Renee would do in front of the cameras followed. By 7 p.m. both Haley and Renee had been signed. They headed home with tickets in hand and prepared to fly to Los Angeles that weekend. Before departing, they gave away most of the possessions they had left, putting only keepsakes and a few irreplaceable items in storage. Less than a week after Haley's initial meeting at the agency, they boarded the plane, still reeling from their luck. Who knew such financial success could find them so quickly?

At LAX, an attractive man with their names on a small white board met them as they exited the revolving door that led to the baggage area. They soon discovered that he was as amiable as everyone else they had met at the agency.

Upon their arrival at the mansion where they would be living, the caretaker collected their identification and passports in case a trip had to be scheduled while they were on a job. "That's what agents do to help their clients," the caretaker explained. It seemed odd at first not to be carrying any ID. But as the days went on, Renee and Haley found that between makeup, wardrobe, photo shoots and other appointments, their schedules were packed so full that they didn't seem to need ID or even money for that matter. The agency paid for all their expenses.

The deal seemed to be getting better and better. The only discordant note was that porn was played much of the time on the house televisions. They were told not to worry. A division of the modeling agency made porn flicks. The divisions, however, were not as separate as initially indicated. Before the week was out, the agency had Haley in nude photo shoots "to build her portfolio and get her comfortable with the cameras." Renee was asked to do some of the risqué photo shoots as well, but because of her age and business experience, they began also training her to recruit other models.

Renee and Haley were disturbed about the porn and uncomfortable with some of the agency requests, but thoughts of their big paychecks at the end of the month made them play along. Payday finally arrived. Mother and daughter opened the envelopes containing their checks with enthusiastic anticipation, only to feel like they'd been blindsided. Neither of them had been paid a dime. Instead, all of their expenses, which the agency had subtracted from their earnings, had been itemized on their pay stubs. Airfare, agent fees, rent, food, transportation, hair, wardrobe, nail salon, makeup and the consultants who told them how to apply it, dress, etc., had all been bought and paid for on their tab. At the end of the first month, both Haley and Renee owed the company more money than they had earned.

When they approached the caretaker in dismay, she told them that the recruiters had explained all this to them. The fact that such a conversation had never taken place didn't alter the bleak reality that now confronted them. The caretaker then reminded the mother and daughter of the contract they had signed, and told them that they were required by law to at least pay back their debt before they could leave, something they later found out was untrue. "The agency has given you so much," the caretaker concluded. "You haven't even allowed yourselves time to make it big. Why, you're still just learning the business!"

When Renee and Haley expressed concern that the bills were adding up faster than the earnings, the caretaker told them there was a way to make greater money, which could get them out of debt. If Haley was willing to act in more nudes and graduate to sexual actions—and possibly even do some escort dates—the agency would increase her wages and her mom's. Renee flatly refused, but Haley stepped forward anyway. "I'll do it," she said. That evening, Renee was called to an impromptu late-night recruiting session so she would not be able to voice her objections as Haley was led off to her first hardcore porn shoot.

Porn Industry Recruitment

The above story was constructed from the real-life experiences of a midwestern mother and daughter who escaped one day when the mom, who was trusted to recruit, accompanied her daughter on a "modeling job." They are currently still in hiding in the Pacific Northwest because they have heard that the agency that recruited them has put out a contract on their lives.

Here are some of the facts about agency techniques that the two documented after making their escape from the industry:[130]

- Agencies typically drop names of major networks, TV shows, and popular men's magazines. It doesn't necessarily mean the agency has any affiliation with anyone associated with the media outlet. It's simply a way to look legitimate to the recruits and draw them in.

- Many young, good-looking men are sent by agencies to college and high school campuses, as well as to parties around the country, to recruit girls, much the same way that pimps recruit victims. Often calling themselves modeling or acting scouts, they use lines like, "Wow, you're so beautiful, you definitely have the looks and body to be a model. I work for a modeling agency in [Miami, New York, Hollywood] and I'd love to submit your photos for some work. I guarantee I can book you solid. I have a couple of companies I work for like [they throw out big name companies at this point to impress] who are looking for a new model with your exact look. You can make $5,000 to $20,000 a month. We will pay all travel expenses and put you up in a five-star hotel while you're there."

- Some of these young recruiters will also pretend to want to date girls they are trying to recruit. If a girl is skeptical, a recruiter may entice her with a whirlwind courtship. Depending on how much the agency wants the girl, significant money may be spent to recruit her. The recruiters have a budget to impress young women, so they rent upscale hotel rooms and fancy cars to make it look like they are successful. For the girls, the relationship turns into what they think is love. For the recruiters, it remains about the money.

- MySpace and Facebook are commonly used to recruit girls. Recruiters work these social networks, which provide them a wealth of information about the potential recruits, including pictures, since many young girls post swimsuit photos on their profiles. Recruiters wait for a status update that indicates that the recruit is emotionally vulnerable (after having had a fight with her mom or boyfriend, for example) then swoop in to offer an attractive alternative.

- Once a girl answers an ad or attends a "casting call," the recruiter convinces her that she's got what it takes to be a star. As soon as the girl believes the hype, the recruiter has her right where he wants her.

- All personal information is gathered, including friends' and family members' names, ages and contact information, financial history and anything else that may be used at a later date to compel the model to stay and comply with what is asked of her.

- Once a new recruit has signed on, she may be given breast implants and other plastic surgery. Agencies don't mention that all the expenses incurred on the model's behalf, including plastic surgery, will have to be paid back to the agency. This isn't revealed until her first paycheck. In typical debt bondage style, once all the expenses have been tallied, she inevitably owes the agency more than she's made, and is told she has to continue to work off that debt before she can leave.

- To earn more money, the model is encouraged to do hardcore porn. Once a girl shoots one of the hardcore scenes, she will almost never qualify for the premium roles they said she was perfect for when they recruited her.

- Another path to higher earnings involves servicing private parties. Wealthy, influential and even political leaders come to private mansions for what are essentially orgies, where drugs and alcohol are plentiful and serving minors is not restricted. Attendees spend large amounts of cash for films of these parties, which are reserved for private viewing, as well as for the privilege of attending the parties in the first place. Of course, the girls themselves usually don't see any of those proceeds, since the money goes directly to the traffickers.

- Once the girl is "modeling," agencies talk about the crossover stars such as Mariah Carey, Sasha Grey, etc., who did nude modeling and then became mainstream movies stars. Even if the shoot is in fact hardcore porn, it is always referred to as modeling.

- As soon as a model has done nude photos, the agency will try to shoot a scene involving her sexual interaction with others. After that has been shot and released, the model will be required to view the footage. The vast majority of models hate watching themselves, so this instills shame and encourages the paranoid belief that everyone has now seen them in porn.

- But the profits don't stop there. Once a girl has made it through the indoctrination process, they cut off her photo shoots. The realization that the other girls in the house have photo shoots and she doesn't causes her to doubt herself. At that point, she is encouraged to do "privates," otherwise known as mainstream prostitution. From then on, the agency plays her like a fiddle, alternating between more porn shots to bring up the price for privates and an increasing amount of work in exotic dancing and forced prostitution.

- The more a girl fights for her independence or limits her shoot types, the harder her traffickers will use and abuse her in order to break her spirit. She may be beaten or used in sadism and masochism (S&M) acts.[131] Don't kid yourselves, the beatings and injuries filmed are real, not staged.[132]

The Damage

Pornography in general—and this kind of violent pornography in particular—is on the rise thanks in large measure to the Internet. Every year brings the release of 13,000 more porn films, which generate $93 billion in annual revenues[133] at the expense of the women and children being sexually exploited on film.

Distribution on the Internet has propelled this turn to "gonzo" pornography, a genre that focuses on "body-punishing sex," to use the words of Gail Dines, author of *Pornland*. This horrific on-screen violence is so pronounced that "there is nothing else to do to a woman's body, outside of killing her," says Dines.[134]

Pornography videos hurt more than just those women and even very young children forced to participate. Fifty percent of the international sex trafficking victims in a 2001 survey said that pornography was used to "educate" them into prostitution.[135] In addition, customers will regularly show the pornography to the sex-trafficked individuals they frequent, so that they can mimic the sex acts performed by the "actress" on the screen.

How will the easy accessibility and increasing frequency of porn in general—and violent porn in particular—influence the sexual behavior of the boys and men who watch it? Only time will tell, but it clearly spreads the message that violence toward women is not only acceptable, it's stimulating. This despite the fact that, as the mother and daughter represented by the Haley and Renee story found out, hardcore porn—including beatings, rapes and other horrific abuses—are used to punish models who try to resist. Again, these acts of violence aren't simulated. They're brutally and disgustingly real.[136]

Help for Those with an Appetite for Porn

It has become more and more evident that the use of pornography has even become common within the Christian community. In March 2005, *Christianity Today* published the results of a study in which 680 pastors were surveyed. Shockingly, "fifty-seven percent said that addiction to pornography is the most sexually damaging issue their congregations have to deal with."[137]

Ted Roberts, author of *Pure Desire* and founder of a ministry of the same name, says, "When I'm at a church speaking about this subject [sexual addiction], 60 to 80 percent of the men with whom I talk admit they're losing this battle."[138] The good news is that there are many resources available for those who find themselves struggling with an attraction to pornography.

In the battle to free oneself from pornography, *Pure Desire* has been recommended by pastors and professionals alike. Additionally, there are many software programs to both guard users from entering porn sites, as well as software programs that will send a report to an accountability partner about websites visited by another computer user.

Money over People

"Pornography…legitimizes the buying and selling of women's bodies," says Dines. And that's big business. According to a 2004 ABC news report, there's more money in porn than in the National Football League, National Basketball Association and Major League Baseball combined.[139] That's understandable when you realize that some of the nation's most recognized corporations profit from bringing porn movies and other productions to the small screen in homes and hotels across the country.

Fighting Fire with Fire

If money is the motivator for the producers of pornography, why not hit them in the wallet? That's part of the rationale behind a recent move toward what is termed a "clean hotel" policy. A company or government entity creates a policy that none of their dollars will be spent for employees to stay in hotels that offer pornography services.

Winona County Minnesota employees, for example, are no longer allowed to stay in hotels that offer pay-per-view pornography. Chuck

Derry, co-founder of the Minnesota Men's Action Network, says Minnesota spent $8 billion in 2005 for costs related to sexual violence, three times what the state spent on costs related to drunken driving. In the meantime, Minnesota hotels collected $500 million in revenues off of their pornography offerings.[140]

Voting with our dollars in this way forces free enterprise to change the way business is done. And that moves all of us forward in terms of recognizing—and reclaiming—each other's humanity.

Going the Extra Step—Engage!

Victims of human trafficking often believe that no one cares about them or their daily suffering. Traffickers and slaveholders are adept at diminishing a person's sense of self worth and convincing their victims that no one really does care. The victims' subsequent belief that no one will help them is often bolstered by their previous deceit and betrayal—sometimes from those close to them. As a consequence, it becomes difficult for victims to trust someone who is really trying to help them. Victims will test anyone trying to help them, and will require continued assurance that the one(s) offering assistance can be trusted and will be willing to make the healing trek with the victim over the long haul.

Again, if you see something that looks like it could be human trafficking, notify law enforcement or call the Trafficking Information and Referral Hotline at 1-888-3737-888. This hotline will help you determine if you have encountered victims of human trafficking. It will also identify resources available in your community to help victims and will help you coordinate with local social service organizations to help protect and serve victims so they can begin the process of restoring their lives. Their website is: http://www.acf.hhs.gov/trafficking/. You can find specific information about sex trafficking at http://www.acf.hhs.gov/trafficking/about/fact_sex.html.

Discussion Questions for Chapter 5

*At one time we too were foolish, disobedient, deceived and enslaved
by all kinds of passions and pleasures.*

—TITUS 3:3

1. Where are some of the places and what are some of the
   methods used by producers of pornography to recruit their
   actors/models/victims?

2. How is debt bondage sometimes used in the production of
   pornography?

3. Discuss the ripple effect of how pornography harms
   all those involved in its production, as well as in its
   consumption.

4. Talk about programs and ways to help someone who is
   hooked on pornography.

5. Locate a recent news story concerning pornography and
   discuss how each and every one of us can help in the fight
   against pornography.

Chapter 6

What's Love Got To Do with It?
Absolutely Nothing!

Prostitution is not the oldest business.
Slavery *is the oldest business.*

—UNKNOWN

The United States is a place where significant sex trafficking takes place, and a large number of domestic minor sex trafficking victims are our own American children. Ernie Allen, in his September 15, 2010 testimony to the U.S. House of Representatives, said of Americans, "Even if they acknowledge that this crime happens in the United States, they assume the victims are foreign children brought into this country who are trafficked only in large cities. In fact, we have learned that most of the victims of domestic minor sex trafficking are American kids who initially leave home voluntarily and are being trafficked on Main Street USA. One police commander said to me, 'the only way not to find this problem in any community is simply not to look for it.'"[141] And unlike drugs or weapons, these slaves are commodities that can be sold over and over again.

"Human traffickers profit by turning dreams into nightmares," says Michael Garcia, U.S. attorney in Manhattan. "These women sought a better life…and found instead forced prostitution and misery."[142] Sadly, the same can be said about thousands of children as well.

A Life Lost

For most of us and for most of our children, turning thirteen and finally becoming a teenager is a time of excitement and anticipation. At that age, I hoped my parents would let me walk to the store or go to a movie or a roller-skating party with my friends without adult supervision. My most grownup "naughtiness" involved sneaking a little eye shadow, passing carefully folded notes to my girlfriends in class and maybe even muttering a swear word when no adult was listening.

For thirteen-year-old Tiffany Mason,[143] life looked much different. She and her twin William had been born to Lori Torres in San Francisco, California in 1986. The eighties were the era where people in the Me, Me, Me generation lived for today and didn't think ten minutes past their nose. As a part of that culture, and as a result of her difficult life, Lori listened more to the drug-addicted monster inside of her than the voice telling her to be a good mother.

By February 1988, her lifestyle and drug addiction had caught up with the young mother. The twins, Tiffany and William, were sent off to live with family in California and Washington State, and were then juggled from relative to relative for the next eleven years. Consistency and roots would never be a part of their childhood. Although Tiffany craved loving, consistent discipline from someone, it was rarely available to her. She once told her cousin Jody Jensen, "I like coming to your house, because you have rules here."[144]

Despite the hard hand she'd been dealt, Tiffany remained positive, always believing life would somehow get better. Meanwhile, the twins' mother Lori continued to live her fast lifestyle until the late nineties when she began sobering up. Finally, in 1999, Tiffany and William were allowed to return to live with the mother they had only been able to visit sporadically. By then Lori had remarried and birthed two additional children. So Tiffany and William shared their new home—room 305 in the West Hotel on Eddy Street in the Tenderloin district of San Francisco—with their mother, her new husband and two toddlers.[145]

The hotel room was no place to reunite with and raise thirteen-year-old twins, and not just because of the lack of space. The Tenderloin district is infamous for its drug addicts, dealers and prostitutes (and combinations thereof). It's not unusual to see people passed out in a doorway, lying in their own urine. It is also known as one of the roughest and most dangerous places for sex-trafficked individuals to walk the "track" (slang for the area where prostitutes and sex-trafficked individuals solicit for customers). Anything goes in the Tenderloin district.

Young Target

Tiffany had just outgrown the stage where many young girls play with dolls and imagine what adult life will be like while playing house. As the friendly youngster who loved to giggle and laugh began to venture out of her hotel room home onto Eddy Street, however, those childhood memories would soon be far behind her. At 4'11", a shapely young woman's figure was already beginning to emerge from her pre-adolescent, more rounded body, and her pretty hazel eyes and wide, bright and innocent smile were endearing. Tragically, a thirteen-year-old virgin is like a neon money sign to the pimps who frequent that area and look for vulnerable young girls to sell, especially since young girls bring more money than older girls because of their young and tender ways.[146]

Before long, Tiffany began coming home with hundred dollar bills. Upon questioning, she confessed to her mom that the money belonged to Damien "Pairadice" Posey,[147] the pimp who allegedly trafficked Tiffany.[148]

Stories of young girls being recruited into forced prostitution by pimps are not as uncommon as one might hope. Twelve to fourteen is the average age that a girl is first turned out for commercial sexual exploitation.[149]

Lori Torres, who worked at Blondies Pizza trying to support her family, could all too readily imagine the danger and trouble ahead for Tiffany if she continued to live in the Tenderloin district. So although she was glad to finally have her children back despite the inevitable stress involved, she immediately relocated the family to Santa Rosa, where she had relatives. Lori and her young family took up residence in a Motel 6, and she found a job waiting tables at the Hungry Hog Restaurant. When DHS learned that Lori had moved to a hotel out of the county, however, they brought the twins back to foster care, placing Tiffany in a group home only ten to fifteen minutes away from the Tenderloin district.

The ninth grader immediately starting staying out late, worrying her foster mother. Then Tiffany began bringing home "gifts" typically given to victims by their pimps, such as stiletto shoes and seductive clothing. In Tiffany's case, those gifts were also accompanied by fresh bruises. Back under Pairadice's control, after just three weeks she threw all her belongings in plastic bags and left in his glossy black Ford Explorer. It should have been no surprise to DHS, or anyone else who understands the dynamics of a girl who has been trafficked, that Tiffany would reconnect with her pimp and quit school, or that he would once again traffic her.

Hindered by the Social Services Designed to Help

Tiffany's mom went to battle for her daughter. She reported what she knew about Pairadice, hoping to prompt his arrest and Tiffany's subsequent release from his grasp.[150] When the authorities did nothing, Lori's hands were tied. "I was homeless, not on drugs. They took away my parental rights and then didn't take responsibility for my kids," says Lori.[151] "I wasn't a good mother. But if you're going to take my kids, then protect them."[152]

A few months later, Pairadice was arrested and Tiffany chose to move back with her mother illegally rather than stay in a group home. But that didn't last long. The twisted, addictive lure of "the life" is strong once a girl has been seasoned and turned out as a sex slave. It is nigh to impossible to explain that unreasonable and insatiable pull, but Tiffany continued to go back, as the majority of girls do. When she was picked up for prostitution, the authorities insisted she be put back in the group home even though they should have suspected that she wouldn't stay.

"The [social services] system sets up a girl to go AWOL," Laurel Freeman, a counselor at the Youth Guidance Center told *Examiner* staff reporter Adrienne Sanders, author of a five-part series titled "Poster Child for Broken Promises." "[The girl] has suffered trauma on the streets. She has a pimp hanging over her. It's easier for them to stick her in a group home—even when they know she's going to run—than it is to come up with something different. It's like a tar pit, miring the girls farther down."[153]

Pairadice knew exactly what to do to maintain his hold on Tiffany. Although she wanted to go back to school, he kept pimping her. He even picked her up in front of Francisco Middle School and later Mission High School, as well as two group homes and the DHS shelter.[154] It was as if those associated with the system allowed pimps like Pairadice the same access as a responsible family member.

He also kept Tiffany away from people who would try to help her break free from the life, and even threatened to kill one shop owner who tried to help her by occasionally buying her a meal or allowing her to sleep on his couch.[155]

Pairadice let her know who was boss. He pulled her hair often—one time even dragging her down the street by her hair. He strangled her. A second pimp called Bautiese "B. Rich" Richardson, a self-proclaimed "Super Pimp" well known for pimping girls who were young like Tiffany, pimped her as well. Amazingly, both men had worked in city youth programs as mentors. B. Rich was also known for his violence against the girls he pimped. After beatings he would tell the girls, "I'm sorry, you know I don't like to hit you."[156]

It is not known how, why, or exactly when Tiffany was shifted back and forth between the pimps like the trump card in a game, but it is a well-known fact that between them they controlled Tiffany's every move. Pimps decide, among other things, where a girl will go, whom she will see and what she will wear. In Tiffany's case, Pairadice decided that her hair would be bleached blonde. "We'll make more scratch [money] that way, Little Momma," he told her. "Dudes dig blondes and you know it."[157]

The life Tiffany lived, as a child whose body was sold multiple times a night on the streets to strangers, was no secret to anyone. Her mother knew and could do nothing to help. Her brother, who was mired in a foster home where the counselors smoked blunts (marijuana-filled cigars) and drank brandy with him and the other foster boys, could do nothing to help.[158] The police knew and would pick her up for prostitution, take her mace and money, and drop her off at the DHS shelter where she was unable to receive the help she needed.

Once when one of her "regular" johns, a forty-nine-year-old man, was caught having sex with Tiffany, he was cited on a misdemeanor of soliciting a prostitute, instead of for statutory rape or child molestation.[159] Actions such as that confirmed and helped Tiffany believe what she had been told repeatedly by Pairadice and others—that she was a "prostitute" and that's all she was good for.

Nobody Should Be a Throwaway

"Protecting johns like this is collusion," says Norma Hotaling, founder of the First Offenders Prostitution Program. "And it gave Tiffany the message that she was a 'toss-away.'"[160] Surprisingly, neither the streets nor the message of worthlessness hardened Tiffany. "Keep your head up," she always told her friends.[161]

Despite her own difficult circumstances, the girl who loved children, especially those with disabilities, still cared about others and did what she could to help them. "Tiffany was a bright spot in my life and she was generous," says her cousin Jody Jensen. During a time when Jensen and her family were surviving on macaroni and cheese, Tiffany came and filled their refrigerator with groceries. Jensen told Tiffany, "I know where you get your money, you don't have to do that, you're a fourteen-year-old little girl." Tiffany helped them out anyway.[162]

Sometimes when I've told her story, people have questioned why Tiffany, as a sex-trafficked girl, occasionally had money to spend or give away. While we know that pimps demand 100 percent of the girls' money, some victims have been known to risk stashing small amounts of cash for a prospective escape or to help a family member as Tiffany did. Tiffany, however, would not get the assistance *she* so obviously needed.

One person, veteran child welfare social worker John Paul Carobus, did his best to help Tiffany, whom he called a "wounded dove."[163] Although he saw what was needed and tried to give her the services she deserved, he met with repeated opposition from his superiors. DHS bureaucrats seemed to be more interested in protecting their own reputations and preventing legal liabilities against themselves and their department than in saving Tiffany's life.

Even so, Carobus made repeated attempts to get Tiffany off the streets. One afternoon he saw her sitting in an outdoor café on Market Street and ran across the street to greet the person he termed "the delightful brat."[164] He bought her lunch and talked to her about leaving the area to go be with some of her family in Santa Rosa where her great-grandmother was celebrating a big birthday. Tiffany initially rejected his advice, but the thought of visiting certain relatives softened her resistance. After expressing embarrassment at them seeing her in what she called "ho clothes," she allowed Carobus to buy her a new outfit at Marshalls that would be more appropriate and to put her on a bus to her relatives.[165]

Knowing her lifestyle and that she was likely to go missing, Carobus asked a passerby to snap a picture of the two of them before she left. He figured with that picture, he could at least have something to put on a missing-child poster when it was needed. One might think that the higher-ups at DHS would applaud such caring actions toward a child so desperately in need of attention. Instead, Carobus was berated in front of his co-workers at a subsequent staff meeting. "I'm giving you a direct order," Carobus' superior told him. "If you see her again you don't go talk to her.... You could be liable."[166] When Tiffany eventually did go missing, Carobus requested permission to print the picture he had taken on a poster to be distributed in the search for her. His request was denied by the City Attorney's office.[167]

Tiffany did not remain in Santa Rosa long. When Lori Torres saw Tiffany in San Francisco on June 5, 2001, she knew her daughter was in trouble and must have wanted to help her in the worst way. She had gone looking for Tiffany, found her on Mission Street and taken her to KFC, where they ate dinner together.[168]

Tiffany knew she was in danger, as well as who was responsible. A few months earlier she had told her mother, "If anything happens to me, Mom, make [Pairadice] pay."[169] After discussing her situation this time around, Tiffany finally relented. "I'll go with you," the girl told her mother. "But I need some cash first. I'll be back in a half hour."

Without any legal rights to detain her own daughter, Torres couldn't stop Tiffany from getting into a shiny black Lexus and leaving. She waited in vain for her return. Torres would never see her daughter alive again.[170]

On July 31st, police picked up Tiffany at 18th and Capp Streets. When their computer check revealed that Tiffany was a missing juvenile, officers dropped her at a DHS shelter. Tiffany called her mom and begged her to come and pick her up. Although she had spent nearly two years turning tricks in forced prostitution for adult pimps, she was still too young to drive. But Torres had no gas and no money. She told her daughter to ask the staff at DHS to put her on a bus home. Later that night, Sprint shut off Lori Torres' cell phone for nonpayment. That was the last conversation she and her daughter would ever have.[171]

The Circuit

Lori would find out after Tiffany's death, that four days after their last conversation on August 3rd Pairadice had driven Tiffany to Sacramento. Pimps often will move their victims from city to city, and even state to state, to minimize the chances of the sex-trafficked individuals successfully reaching out for help. In the process, they provide variety for their clients and escape detection by law enforcement agents.[172] After a couple of weeks, they relocate them to the next place. "The bottom line is that they keep moving, especially [when] a child is [involved]," says Keith Bickford, head of the Oregon Human Trafficking Task Force. "If a kid leaves foster care and ends up with a pimp, that kid is gone…within a couple hours. We've found them down in Las Vegas and we've found them up in Seattle."[173] Along the way, truck stops provide seasoning for newly turned-out victims and plenty of clients to pad the money clips of pimps.

The objective is to keep the trafficked individual producing income, no matter what. If she looks like she's on the verge of getting help, she's moved. And if she gets pregnant, that's taken care of too. Forced abortions are not uncommon among sex-trafficked individuals. It makes no difference to the pimp if she wants to keep her child. One Mexican girl who had been trafficked across the border complained about terrible vaginal pain to no avail. "I asked repeatedly to be taken to the doctor. No one ever took me," she recalled. "But they did take the girls who became pregnant to a doctor where they performed forced abortions."[174]

The sex slave's health and wellbeing is simply not an issue. Neither is her safety, as Tiffany's story shows in heartbreaking detail. Tiffany was killed on August 4th, the day after being driven to Sacramento. Her pimp, Pairadice, remembers seeing her cross Stockton Boulevard and get into the car of a john. Five days later, a fisherman reported catching sight of a corpse drifting slowly with the current in Lake Natoma. Folsom police cast a large net and dragged out Tiffany's nude body. She had been floating face down in a sitting position, her head bashed and her long beautiful hair, still bleached blonde, tangled in twigs. Local campers, park rangers, law enforcement personnel and medical examiners stood and watched the operation from the shoreline. Security officers stood guard on the edge of the crime tape to keep the public and reporters at bay.[175]

Carobus, the social worker who had tried on many occasions to help Tiffany, had been denied permission to print the picture he had taken of her on the Missing Child poster because California law states that the child's confidentially can't be broken. "Tiffany's confidentiality certainly was broken when she was floating in the lake," he remarked bitterly when her body was found.[176]

It is not known how many sex-trafficked youngsters, like Tiffany, are murdered by a john. They're usually estranged from their families, so their relatives might not even know and be able to report that they're missing.

"They're not going to file a missing person's report," a former pimp I interviewed told me.[177] "They assume, 'Oh she's probably out doing something bad somewhere and nobody really knows where she is.'" Pimps won't report a girl missing—or even check with the family to see if she has run home—because the finger will be pointed towards them. Besides, according to pimps, the girls are expendable. "There's a big window of opportunity for girls to become victims [without anyone knowing]," the pimp told me. "It could be months to years before they're ever found." If they're found at all.

Where the Men Are

As we've seen over and over again, human traffickers value profit over life. It's all about the money. As a result, individuals who have been sex-trafficked not only are forced to work the circuit (the city-to-city trek around which the pimps move the girls for reasons previously stated), they're routinely brought into areas hosting big events that cater to a primarily male population. And in that category, there's none bigger than football's Super Bowl, with spending in the locale hosting the event ranging from $150 million to a record-setting $195 million during the Super Bowl played in South Florida in 2007.[178] Couple that kind of money with the accompanying party culture and you have a traffickers' playground, according to Pastor Brad Dennis, the director of Search Operations for the KlaasKids Foundation, who also oversees the Gulf Coast Coalition Against Human Trafficking.[179]

To usher in Super Bowl XLIV in Miami, a local free publication featured a scantily clad blonde on the front cover with the large caption that read: "Super Blow." Inside was a how-to manual for those rookies looking to buy sex and drugs. The article advertised, "You can have anything you want for the right price. Down here, there's a general understanding that everybody needs something."[180] It went on to say that one could "hire prostitutes of eight races and three sexual orientations, and find a group of people willing to dress up like horses and let you whip them all before dinner." In case the reader was looking for more detailed information, the article also offered information on how to determine if your prostitute was a cop, decode escort ads, behave in strip clubs, and retrieve the most enjoyment for your money. Accompanying paid advertisements ensured that Super Bowl tourists would be provided with whatever their hearts desired. If there was ever any question that the Super Bowl was culturally connected with illegal sex and drugs, this publication erased all wonder.

The single positive aspect of such seediness is the opportunity that this yearly convergence of human traffickers presents for rescuing victims. Which is why in February 2010, I joined Brad Dennis as well as Anna Rodriguez, founder and CEO of Florida Coalition Against Human Trafficking, to do an outreach to girls being sexually trafficked in Miami during the Super Bowl.

Armed with missing children flyers, several of us spent daytime hours canvassing businesses where pimps might bring their girls, including a flea market with a plethora of cheap nail and hair salons, tattoo parlors, and lingerie shops.

When I walked into one tattoo booth and sat the clipboard I had with the missing girls' pictures on the glass case in front of us, the manager teared up and turned her head. As she composed herself and began looking at the flyers, she recognized several of the girls. We gathered as much detailed information from her as we could and expressed our gratitude. Solid leads like the ones she provided were turned over to the local authorities and became key in recovering many missing and endangered kids that weekend.

During the nights, we walked the streets of South Beach in Miami, which literally crawled with sex-trafficked individuals and their pimps. Our challenge was to find those juveniles made to dress up and work as sex slaves.

These children being trafficked have been abused, raped and manipulated into believing this is all their idea, that this is a choice they are making. And yet our society has labeled them "willing participants in a victimless crime." What a tragedy. These are children being used in the most horrific ways to make money for pimps, who are often their "boyfriends," with whom they believe they are in love. Considering the brainwashing and sexual abuse these girls have experienced at the hands of their pimps, it is a wonder they have survived.

The truth is that many have not. According to one study, 65 percent of female sex trafficking victims reported suffering internal pain, 24 percent experience head injuries, and 12 percent report broken bones.[181] And since so many of the missing never get reported, we'll never know just how many lose their lives.

It's Everywhere

The Super Bowl and other big events are not prerequisites for such human trafficking. Sexual exploitation of human trafficking victims is happening in cities, towns and rural areas all over this fair country of ours. America is the richest nation in the world. It stands to reason that traffickers milk the land of plenty, where they can reap the biggest profits.

To be sure, not all prostitutes have been trafficked. But most women in prostitution are doing it against their will,[182] with 89 percent of those prostitutes surveyed in nine countries wanting to escape prostitution.[183]

The advent of the Internet and a growing demand hasn't helped them. Instead of those women who want a different life being released, more are being brought in. Using the Internet to connect johns with sex—a huge and fast-growing method for the "marketing" of victims—provides johns with anonymity as well as relatively easy access to nearly anything sexual that anyone could possibly want. "The Internet serves as a virtual clearinghouse, a sex bazaar connecting demand and supply," wrote one observer.[184]

This use of the Internet to connect johns with prostitutes, many of whom are victims of human trafficking, isn't limited to Internet porn websites or other sexually-oriented pages. Shockingly, traffickers and pimps frequent many well known Internet sites with legitimate uses—sites such as MySpace, Facebook, and others—both to recruit women and children and to sell them to johns who know how to find what they are looking for sexually by surfing the 'net. And that has substantially broadened the numbers of children now at risk.

As we've already discussed, as of the writing of this book, Craigslist had just promised to discontinue their Adult Services ads within the United States for good. It is estimated by the *New York Times* that those discontinued ads would have brought in $44 million to Craigslist in 2010.[185] While Craigslist succumbing to public pressure is good news, this is a drop in the bucket. Children and adults continue to be marketed online as sexual commodities. Still, it does prove that we as the public have the power to pressure businesses into cleaning up their acts.

We have a long way to go, since in addition to connecting buyers to sex-trafficked individuals, the Internet also facilitates the trafficking of women from foreign countries into the United States through "marriage" to American men who use online mail-order bride services. Most mail-order brides coming to America have little understanding of their basic rights and therefore are too often abused, sexually exploited, and recruited or coerced into prostitution almost as soon as they set foot on American soil. "I didn't plan to go in for prostitution," said one such woman. "I just wanted to be a wife."[186]

Sex Tourism

Sex tourism, defined as traveling to a foreign country with the intent to engage in sexual activity with a child, has become another unfortunate part of American human trafficking. It is illegal for a U.S. citizen to engage in such activity, and prosecutable under the TVPA. The fact that it's illegal does not stop it from happening. American sex tourism is also prevalent in a number of other countries, including Cambodia, where Americans make up 38 percent of that country's sex tourists, and in Costa Rica, where Americans comprise 80 percent of their sex tourism visitors.[187] Overall, it is estimated that Americans comprise about 25 percent of all sex tourists around the world.[188]

Johns justify their actions by saying they are giving money to children who are being sold for sex so the children and their families can eat, or that sex is not looked upon the same way in many foreign cultures. Both of those arguments are empty. Sex tourism is just another form of human trafficking. Just as with any other form of human trafficking, the perpetrator is the one profiting, not the victims or their families. Also, we must never downplay the fact that paid sex disregards the humanity of the victim, and is horrifically damaging to the victim in any culture.

Warning: It *Can* Happen to Your Kids

Americans, however, certainly don't have to travel to buy sex. Even sex with a child or young adult is readily available right in their communities. Our American daughters and sons, natural born U.S. citizens, make up the largest portion of minor sex trafficking victims in the U.S.[189] Though statistics regarding the number of children like Tiffany or Sarah, who you met earlier in this book, aren't clear, we do know that *the average age range of a child first forced into prostitution is eleven to fourteen, with some as young as nine years of age, according to FBI assistant director Chris Swecker.*[190]

It is difficult for most people, especially those who grew up in fairly "normal" families, to understand that teenage girls from families like yours and mine regularly fall for the tactics pimps use. "When they hear the term 'child trafficking,' most Americans think that it only happens somewhere else, in Southeast Asia or Central America," reads Ernie Allen's written testimony presented to the U.S. House of Representatives.[191]

Unfortunately, some in our country appear determined to believe just that. One day I talked to an educator, who seemed to take the position that human trafficking wasn't a problem in middle-class America.[192] He struck me as someone who considered human trafficking to be a political problem more than a national and international crisis that affects real people—even our own daughters, sisters, sons, and brothers. I also realized that this man didn't understand just how widespread and pervasive the danger of human trafficking in the United States really is. So I asked him, "What if one of your daughters, when she becomes a teenager, is lured into being friends with an online predator—on Facebook, MySpace, or X-Box Live—and that predator talks her into meeting him, and she becomes a victim?"

His answer reaffirmed my belief that one of the biggest obstacles to stopping human trafficking in the United States is that people don't believe it can happen to them or to their loved ones. "She's not vulnerable, because we don't live in poverty," he answered. "It's not possible because we are middle class, not poor. This is about poverty."[193]

This kind of thinking concerns me. While it's true that traffickers and pimps prey much more often on the underprivileged and economically vulnerable than on those in the middle classes and above, the simple truth is that under certain circumstances, anyone, regardless of her economic and social status, can fall into the hands of traffickers and pimps. We saw that in the opening story in this book about Sarah.

Brad Dennis understands just how common this "it can't happen to my kids" thinking really is, even among people with knowledge about human trafficking and slavery.

"Those who think that way are only kidding themselves," he said. "I hear that thought process all the time—that the girls out there on the streets being prostituted don't have much of a choice anyway, they don't have much of a life anyway—they're ghetto girls, they're trailer park girls. I've heard it from ministries, I've heard it from law enforcement, I've heard it from social services, and I've heard it from non-government organizations who were supposed to be involved."[194] But people who buy into that thinking, he told me, are living in a world of false security.

Preying on the Weak

Pimps and traffickers know how to sniff out and exploit vulnerability, and not just the kind that comes from living in situations of poverty, neglect, and abuse. They know that in many cases just being a typical teenager can make any young girl vulnerable.

As the mother of two grown children, I understand how even those teenagers who grow up in solid Christian homes go through times of insecurity, times when they want to experience new things and push against the boundaries and limitations their parents place on them. In addition, even the most well-balanced, emotionally happy teen living in a loving, affirming home can go through seasons when she believes (often wrongly) that she is not loved or appreciated at home or liked at school. These typical feelings and emotional stages in the lives of healthy, normal teens make them vulnerable to human trafficking predators.

Yes, pimps are predators. The very nature of the word *predator* should give us a good idea of how pimps operate. Every spring in central Oregon, people begin to venture into the woods to hike, camp, and fish. During that time of year, local television channels broadcast news spots instructing the public about what to do if they encounter a cougar in the woods: "Anyone spotting a cougar should take certain steps—don't run, but make a noise and appear as large as possible. Open your coat if you have one. Raise your arms, but do not turn your back. If attacked, fight back and use whatever might be available. Always keep children and pets close by when hiking in cougar habitat."[195]

Cougars, like most predatory wild animals, can spot vulnerability. If the cougar sees a small human, a child, it is likely to attack because it knows that it can win the fight. An adult who curls up in a ball upon coming into visual contact with a cougar is likely to be attacked because he or she has become small and defenseless.

The same principle holds true with traffickers/pimps. They aren't guided by any sense of morality or right and wrong, only by the feeling that they can overpower certain targets. Of course, when it comes to young children, they don't even have to fight to claim their prize.

Easy Pickings

Arturo*[196] did what he always did when he was nervous or bored or afraid. As the van bounced along the rough Mexican road, he ran his brown calloused fingers over the rosary that belonged to his mother. He was excited and nervous to be going with Marco*, a twenty-something Mexican-American who had offered him a new life in America and a job. Not only was the salary good, his duties would include being an extra in the movies. Once when he was twelve, he had gone to see a movie with his friends. He had heard of movie stars and the life of luxury they lived, and dreamed of having his own house, plenty of food and even a shiny black sports car with flashy chrome wheels.

When his mother was alive, they had taken care of one another. She would often sing to him as he was going to sleep at night and he would think of funny jokes to make her smile. He had never known his father and he had grown up feeling like the man of the house. He knew how to work hard and raise everyone's spirits.

He had loved to see his mother's smile, so it bothered him that now, just a few months after her death, he sometimes had trouble remembering her face. He promised her he would never forget her and would make her proud.

Since his mother's death, he had taken odd jobs handing out flyers for a promotional company to earn enough money for food. He had been hired partially because of his good looks and charm, which seemed to be an asset that opened doors for him. But now he had the opportunity to live up to his deathbed promise. He rubbed the beads of the rosary between his fingers and thought of how proud she would be of him going to America all by himself at only fourteen years of age.

Arturo slept through the night in the van traveling to America, his stomach no longer aching with hunger because Marco had fed him tortillas, as well potato chips and cookies. As daylight broke and they neared the Tijuana border, the boy wondered if they would really let him cross. He had heard stories of others who had paid large sums to come to America and had been turned away at the border. Marco told him that after he arrived, he would only have to pay back his transportation costs with his earnings, which wouldn't take long with the great job he was about to get.

At the border station, a man with a gruff voice asked Marco for their papers, which Marco quickly produced. Soon they were speeding along the freeway on the American side of the border. Arturo gazed out in absolute amazement at the Southern California homes they passed. Riches seemed to be everywhere. He was going to have a better life than he had even dreamed.

When they got to Oceanside, Marco took him to a house with boarded up windows in a neighborhood much nicer than the ones he had known in Mexico, though not as nice as the houses they had passed along the way. As they walked inside the front door with four deadbolts, Marco spoke with a man named Tito*. After some argument about price, Marco accepted some money from Tito and left Arturo with him.

There were two other boys and also two girls living in the house, all four near Arturo's age. He was happy to meet other kids, but they seemed to be very guarded in all their actions and spoke very few words. One boy, Martin*, seemed friendlier than the others, almost as if he wanted a friend as much as Arturo did. They exchanged names and nervous glances.

Nighttime came and the children were all allowed a small portion of beans and rice from the big meal they had prepared for the adults who lived there. It wouldn't be long before Arturo found out why the children seemed so afraid.

Just after dark, Tito began opening the door to various men. Arturo was told to sit on the couch with the other children as the men looked them over. The first man took one of the girls in the other room. A few minutes later Martin was told to go with a man into the next room.

As Martin shuffled off in a room with the man, another unshaven American man with gray in his red-colored beard and hair, pointed to Arturo. The boy was told to stand up and turn in a circle so the man could see him front and back. When the man nodded his head, Arturo was told to go to the back bedroom with him.

What happened in that room could only be described as worse than Arturo's worst nightmare. Arturo fought the man's advances to no avail. After the rape, Arturo scrambled to get his clothes back on and curled up in a fetal position on the bed. Tito came in within a few minutes and hit him across the face with an open fist. "Quit being a baby and get out on the couch," he demanded. There were more customers to serve. The small amount of rice and beans came up Arturo's throat as he took a quick detour to the bathroom.

Arturo serviced three other customers that night. His body screamed in pain by the time he fell asleep just before dawn. He had heard of places like this, but never dreamed he would be trapped in such a hellhole. And trapped he was. With the windows boarded and the doors locked, he barely saw daylight. He understood now that there was no promotional job, no acting as a movie extra. Instead, he had been brought here to "work" in this brothel.

Martin seemed to understand what Arturo was feeling and offered an occasional understanding smile. He even helped Arturo with his daytime chores of scrubbing the baseboard and floors. As the months went on, the two boys developed as much of a friendship as was allowed. Although Arturo would never get used to the men raping him as they did every night, the friendship with Martin made it bearable.

During that time, however, Tito became more and more violent. He had frequently threatened Arturo with his big knife. One Thursday evening, he actually used it. While cooking the evening meal for Tito and his friends, Arturo had accidently burned some of the potatoes. Tito was furious. In the beating that ensued, he cut Arturo's thigh almost to the bone. The wound bled so much that Tito realized it was going to need stitches. He called a friend who was a nurse to sew up the wound. As the gentle man carefully stitched and dressed the wound, Arturo thought this might be a way out. But his hopes were soon dashed when he was required to give the nurse "payment" for this medical service. It seemed that no one would help him, and the severe pain in his leg matched the hopelessness in his heart.

As the months wore on, he and Martin dreamed together of a time they could live in the "America, Land of the Free" they had been promised. They wondered aloud how long they could endure the nightly shame and pain and being enslaved in this prison. Martin had been there longer than Arturo and had started younger. It seemed like their incarceration and sexual exploitation was harder on him than on any of the kids. Despite the comfort he took in Arturo's friendship, he began to withdraw. Arturo knew the life was getting the better of his closest friend.

It had been a particularly rough week for all the kids. In addition to increasing numbers of customers, Tito was drinking more and more. At 4:00 a.m., the customers finally quit coming for the night. Arturo noticed that his friend Martin had been in the bathroom for some time and decided to check on him. He opened the door a crack, then saw the blood covering the floor and splattered all over the sink, cabinet, tub, and toilet. As fear gripped him, he pushed open the door. Martin lay in a pool of his own blood, without breath, without pulse. As Arturo screamed his friend's name over and over again, the other children came rushing in, followed by Tito.

Tito picked up Martin's body, roughly shoving it under one arm. As Martin's hair flicked blood on the carpet and walls, Tito lugged his limp body down the hallway and gruffly barked orders to the other children to clean up the mess. "I'd better not be able to see one drop of Martin's filthy blood when I return," he ordered.

The next two years were harder for Arturo. He had lost his only friend in the world, and had learned in the process not to allow himself to get close to—or to feel for—the others. He kept to himself and survived by pretending he was someone else, somewhere else, when the nightly rapes occurred. Sometimes he wondered whether he should end it all as Martin had done. The memory of Martin's blood always stopped him from following through.

One particularly hot and humid day, after Tito and his cohorts had consumed plenty of drugs and liquor while celebrating a birthday, Tito opened one of the high windows in the kitchen so that a fresh breeze would blow through the house. He then continued to party. Eventually, the men passed out and the children saw their first chance to escape. Arturo and Victor*, the boy who had replaced Martin, wriggled through the open window. They tried to pull the two girls through the opening, but couldn't manage to get them out. When Tito awoke and began to yell, the two boys ran.

Arturo and Victor had no idea where they were going, but knew they never wanted to go back to that house. So they forced themselves to keep running even when they felt they could go no farther. They were convinced that if Tito found them, they would be killed. On the outskirts of Oceanside, they found a park where many homeless and illegal aliens gathered. There Arturo was befriended by a couple. Eventually when he came to trust them, he told them about his horrific ordeal of coming to America.

The caring couple sought out options for Arturo, and found a place for him across the country at the Florida Coalition Against Human

Trafficking (FCAHT), where he received shelter, counseling, education and acceptance. His caseworker there, Giselle Rodriguez, cared for him in genuine ways and believed in him. Although his trauma was great, little by little the healing began.

Arturo is now nineteen years old and is currently attending school to become a social worker. After experiencing support from FCAHT, he wants to help others who may have experienced hard lives to overcome their issues the way he has.

He carries regret that will last a lifetime about being forced to leave the girls at the brothel that night. Because he couldn't provide the police with the location of the house once he finally learned to trust the authorities, nothing was ever done about the operation, and to his knowledge the other kids were never rescued.

Wanted: Future Sex Slaves

From the malls to Facebook, kids and young women are daily targets for human traffickers looking to exploit them sexually. When confronted by these skilled veterans who excel at molding their message, uninformed targets rarely have a chance. "What you can see, time and time again, is that the predators will adapt their means to whatever the young people are doing—whether its malls, whether its ski slopes, whether its beaches," FBI Deputy Assistant Director Chip Burrus says. "Predators…are going to do everything in their power to try to convince young girls and young boys to come with them and enter this particular lifestyle."[197]

The pimp paints a scenario for the youngsters that minimizes or denies the realities of sex trafficking. He may tell his recruit that others are giving it away for free, or that while everyone gets something for sex—like clothes, dinner, a home—she will get straight cash. (Never mind the fact that *all* of that cash comes back to the pimp.) He may also play down the fact that she's selling herself and selling her soul, telling her instead that having sex for money is just like waiting tables, doing plumbing, or counseling someone. She's not really selling herself, he tells her. She's just providing a service.

Turning Out—Initiation

Every sex-trafficked individual—no matter how young or how old—has a story. Each story is unique, and yet many have tremendous similarities. Each involves a recruitment of sorts, followed by a seasoning when one is turned out. The object of this methodology is to eradicate the victim's identity, deleting any personal self-worth and triggering the abandonment of any sense of entitlement when it comes to dignity, bodily integrity or choices in life. The seasoning may include exerting control via rapes, beatings, starvation, and taking pornographic photos of the victim that can be used as blackmail, fortifying the pimp's story that she has voluntarily chosen to be in the sex trade. Isolation from family and friends makes it easier to control her. Then, stripped of any sense of self-esteem, the victim learns obedience to the man who has broken her and to anyone he designates as his surrogate.

Dissociation

After being broken in or turned out—and learning her place in the process—a trafficked girl or young woman adopts the identity forced upon her and loses any sense of her own humanity and worth. Small wonder. As Vednita Carter and Evelina Giobbe write in the *Hastings Women's Law Journal*: "A girl who enters prostitution at fourteen will have submitted to the sexual demands of four thousand men before she is old enough to drive a car, eight thousand men before she is old enough to vote, and twelve thousand men before she is deemed mature enough to buy a single beer in many states."[198]

It seems that people around the world forced into prostitution share similar coping mechanisms. In her book *Prostitution, Trafficking and Traumatic Stress*, Melissa Farley quotes an Australian victim who says, "When I work my face is expressionless. Of course when I first speak to them, I put on my best pretty-please smile. But in the room I become nothing and nobody. I can only work from below the neck. If I have to think about a service or involve my mind even slightly, I feel dirty. I avoid fantasies. I don't want to participate in their filth."[199]

The message was eerily similar when "Today Show" anchor Meredith Vieira asked Katya*, a survivor of sex trafficking who was trafficked from an Eastern Bloc country to Detroit, what she wanted people to understand about trafficking. "We was really scared. There was physical abuse on us and they tell us the story about other girls who escape, they bombed their cars, and I was just really scared for my life and my mom's life…I want them to understand, if I have a smile on my face, it doesn't mean I'm here with my own will," she said. "It doesn't mean that I appreciate this job and I want to be here, [but] that it's not for me just easy to leave because I was kept [against my will]."[200]

Tragically, rescue is a hit-and-miss business for victims in the U.S., something we'll revisit in the next chapter. But for victims of reverse trafficking—a new trend involving American citizens trafficked to another country—odds of rescue are even slimmer. Florida Coalition Against Human Trafficking's Anna Rodriguez told me that American girls respond to newspaper classified ads promising modeling, singing or dancing jobs abroad, only to find out once they arrive in the foreign country that the jobs don't exist.[201] Instead, they're forced into sex trafficking in strip clubs or brothels to repay their debts.

One young dancer from Las Vegas[202] answered an ad touting a musical in Japan, applied and got hired. She would have to leave her three-year-old child behind, but the experience and the money she would be able to bring home would make the two or three months of separation worthwhile.

Instead of the theatrical break she anticipated, however, upon her arrival she was taken to a home where she was beaten and gang raped for a week and a half. Once her traffickers had broken her will, they put her to work in their brothel. The group that now controlled her said that in order for her to be free, she had to repay all the money they had spent to bring her over. It took her three years to save the required amount. That's when they told her that she had not accounted for the interest and now owed them more.

Luckily, shortly thereafter an open window provided an avenue for escape, and eventually she was able to make her way back to the United States.[203]

Pain, Not Pleasure

Despite the realities, the myth persists that the prostitute, the stripper, the porn star is there because she chooses or wants to be. Most of the time, this impression of the "wanton woman" is completely false. Usually she has been subjected to someone else's evil and violent deeds, and forced to do what she does.

In truth, even the woman who isn't a victim of human trafficking—at least as I've defined it in this book—but who sells her body to strangers doesn't enjoy it. In the overwhelming majority of these instances, the women who "work" in prostitution and pornography do so not because it is some kind of chosen career path, but simply because they have to eke out a living and don't believe they have alternatives.

That's just one reason why the arguments to legalize prostitution don't hold water. Legalized prostitution benefits only the pimps, brothels and johns. Amsterdam, a tourist destination in part because of its long-term legal prostitution, has attracted sex traffickers in droves. It might also surprise you to learn that sexual harassment becomes more common in areas with a high density of sex businesses.[204] Indeed, Nevada's rate of rape in 2004 was 40.9 per 100,000, higher than the U.S. average (32.2) and significantly higher than many other states.[205]

Finally, Nevada's legalization of prostitution actually encourages sex

trafficking instead of eliminating it. In its report of January 2007, the
U.S. Department of Justice named Las Vegas one of the seventeen most
likely destinations for sex trafficking victims.[206]

Despite what the popular ad says, what happens in Las Vegas (and
places like it) does not stay in Vegas. Sex trafficking is a stain on humanity
and hurts us all. But please don't judge those victims, even when they stay
in ugly situations they never sought. If you had been subjected to what
they have, you might too.

Get Political

In addition to helping the victims we encounter in our everyday lives, we
need to help keep the multitude of potential and future victims safe. That
means lobbying politicians for laws that effectively fight sex trafficking.
Many of the laws currently on the books punish the victims—the very
people who have been trafficked—instead of the perpetrators who pimp
them.

Compare that to Sweden. In 1999, the country changed its laws to
criminalize the purchase of sexual services. Instead of punishing the victims, as we do in this country, those who profit from sex trafficking are
incarcerated for up to ten years, and those who support it as customers
are slapped with fines and/or jail sentences of up to six months. The
victims themselves are funneled into social services to get the help they
clearly need. By October 2004, five years after the law's enactment, street
prostitution had reportedly decreased by at least 30 to 50 percent, and
the recruitment of new women for street prostitution had plummeted to
almost nothing.[207]

Our legal system has begun to recognize that the majority of prostituted individuals are or have been victims and that the real criminals are
the pimps, along with the largely male johns who come from all walks
of life, reflect every race, are young and old, rich and poor, married and
single. In 2009, for example, Sheriff Tom Dart of Cook County, Illi-

nois directed his department to model Sweden's system. Accordingly, resources previously directed at the repeated cycle of arresting, releasing and re-arresting those practicing prostitution have been shifted to target the crime's perpetrators instead. Local law enforcement now arrests pimps and johns and impounds their cars.[208]

Prostituted individuals, instead of being incarcerated, are referred to social services for support and assistance, so they can recover physically, emotionally and financially from the traumatic and inhumane experiences they have suffered. They need the help. A study by the Chicago Coalition for the Homeless revealed that of 235 women in Cook County Jail on October 31, 2001, "82 percent of the women had been physically assaulted; 83 percent had been threatened with a weapon, [and] 68 percent had been raped while working as a prostitute."[209] The 2005 Trafficking in Persons Report stated that 70 to 95 percent of women in prostitution were physically assaulted.[210]

While not perfect, I believe that moves such as this one will be key in the efforts to stop the sale of humans in the United States.

Discussion Questions for Chapter 6

Everyone who saw it said, "Such a thing has never been seen or done,
not since the day the Israelites came up out of Egypt.
Think about it! Consider it! Tell us what to do!"

—JUDGES 19:30

1. The material in this chapter is possibly the most disturbing in this book. Feeling sad and disturbed about the material is a normal reaction. If you are reading this book as a group study, discuss your feelings with your group. If you are reading this book alone, find a friend or relative with whom to discuss your feelings.

2. As a group, read Judges 19, from which the scripture above was taken. Discuss how this biblical story parallels some of the stories we've seen in this chapter.

3. Tiffany Mason is a sad example of how young teens who have been sex trafficked are dying. Look for an organization working to help these young teens and discuss how you might assist them through prayer or financial support or by volunteering your time.

4. As of the writing of this book, the Adult Services section of Craigslist has been shut down due to consumer pressure. What are some other ways that we as consumers may bring pressure upon businesses to help stop sex trafficking?

5. Find a recent news story about someone rescued from sex trafficking and discuss it.

Chapter 7

Why Victims Stay

If I could have convinced more slaves that they were slaves,
I could have freed thousands more.

— Harriet Tubman

August 23, 1973, began like any other day for Kristin Enmark, a petite twenty-three-year-old[211] woman with short sassy brown hair from Stockholm, Sweden. She had already plunged into her work as a bank stenographer, a job she generally liked, when she heard a commotion out in the lobby area. She looked up to see a man with an afro wig and sunglasses pull out a machine gun, which he fired in the air. She and the forty other terrified bank employees and customers ducked for cover or ran out of the bank.

"The party has only started," the man shouted in English.[212]

Police were called and responded quickly. As they walked into the bank, the gunman, Jan-Erik Olsson, shot and injured one of the two policemen. He ordered the other officer to sit in a chair and "sing something." The officer managed to croak out a few bars of "Lonesome Cowboy."[213]

Olsson, who had intended to rob the bank, took hostage four bank employees—three women (Kristin, Birgitta Lundblad and Elizabeth

123

Oldgren) and one man (Sven Safstrom). He ordered a male bookkeeper to tie their hands behind their backs. He made several demands of police, including that they bring a friend of his, Clark Olofsson, from prison where he was serving a sentence for another crime.[214]

Kristin would later learn that in addition to the machine gun, Olsson had brought reserve ammunition, plastic explosives (which he had expertise in using), blasting caps, a knife, and a radio. He meant business. Even though he had botched the bank robbery, he remained determined to make something out of what was left.[215]

Over the next days, Kristin and the other hostages would come to know Olsson and Olofsson not only as strangers who held the key to their life and death, but as the men who controlled everything about their lives, including where and what they ate, where and how much they slept, where and when they went to the bathroom and how safe they felt.

Curiously, in short order this also gave the gunmen control over their hostages' emotions. In a matter of hours, Kristin and the others had so bonded to the gunmen that they believed the two men were actually protecting them from law enforcement, which they now viewed as a threat. Further, the hostages had become protective of the gunmen, whom they viewed as saviors rather than captors. The phenomenon would become known as "The Stockholm Syndrome."[216] [217]

For five days, as the hostages were trapped in the bank vault with their captors, they had explosives strapped to them, witnessed the robbers shoot two more officers who were trying to rescue them by drilling a hole in the top of the bank vault, and had their lives threatened daily.[218] Yet by the second day of captivity, when Olsson gave a commissioner permission to come in and check on the welfare of the hostages, the hostages showed hostility toward the commissioner. He said that none of the hostages had any requests for him and he could detect no imploring looks. There seemed to be a cordial disposition between the hostages and their captors; Olofsson even stood with his arm around Kristen and Elisabeth's shoulders in seeming camaraderie. To Kristin, who practically curled up her lip at the commissioner, the disdain she felt toward him made perfect sense. His presence jeopardized the safety she felt with Olsson and Olofsson.

Officials had agreed to almost all of Olsson's requests, including bullet-proof jackets, food, money, two pistols, and a fast getaway car. The only non-negotiable item was that the captors not be allowed to take the hostages with them if they left, even though all four had petitioned to leave with their captors.[219]

Later that day, Kristin had the opportunity to call the Prime Minister, Olof Palme. Although she didn't know him personally, they spoke for forty-two minutes. She felt that if she could convince him that they were really safe here with Olsson, the officials would let them all leave together.

"I am really disappointed," she told the Prime Minister. "I think you are sitting there playing checkers with our lives. I fully trust Clark [Olofsson] and the robber [Olsson]. I am not desperate. They haven't done a thing to us. On the contrary, they have been very nice. But you know, Olof, what I'm scared of is that the police will attack and cause us to die."[220]

"The police will not harm you," the Prime Minister replied. "Can you believe that?"

"You must forgive me, but in this situation I don't believe it."

"I think that's terribly unfair. Here are a great many policemen risking their lives, who have not moved aggressively in all this time. The purpose, of course, is to protect you."

"Of course they can't attack us…[Olsson] is sitting here and he's protecting us from the police."

The phone call ended with Kristin sarcastically telling Prime Minister Palme, "Thanks for the help!"[221]

Kristin and the other hostages were fully convinced by the second day that their safety was dependent on the robbers, not the police.

The third day, after negotiations to have the police send in food and other supplies had fallen through, Olsson wrote the following note:

"The girls have begun to believe that police intend to sacrifice them and are only looking for an excuse to justify the massacre later on. The girls believe that the police will make sure it was we who started it and that the police simply defended themselves, so that they can afterward regret that everyone was killed."[222]

Later when the ordeal was over, another hostage, Birgitta Lunblad, was asked if the note was accurate. She indicated it was. "We were facing two threats, and one was all we could possibly handle. About the robber's threat we could do nothing—he was armed and we were with him. But we weren't with the police. We imagined we could protect ourselves against them. To imagine that, of course, meant believing in Jan [Olsson]."[223]

Kristin and Olofsson formed a special bond. One night she awoke from a nightmare screaming, "Don't! Don't!" Olofsson immediately rushed to her side, consoling her until she was herself again. She told police after the rescue that she and Olofsson held hands. "Perhaps it sounds a little like a cliché but Clark [Olofsson] gave me tenderness…. It made me feel enormously secure. It was what I needed."[224]

Even at the end of the ordeal, after five days in the vault, Kristin tried to defend her captors as they were to exit. Police had sprayed tear gas in the vault causing choking and vomiting inside.

"We give up, let us out!" Olsson hollered.[225]

"Hostages first," the police replied.

Kristin refused. "No, Jan [Olsson] and Clark [Olofsson] go first. You'll gun them down if we [leave first]," she yelled.[226]

As the vault door was opened, the hostages and their captors said their goodbyes. The women kissed their captors, and the male hostage shook their hands. Then all six came out of the vault, perpetrators first.

The hostages were to be taken to a medical center to be evaluated. Kristin, however, was so worried about the men who had taken her hostage that she refused to lay on her stretcher. As she craned her neck to see them and spotted Olofsson being interrogated by police, she called out, "Clark, I'll see you again!"[227] And she did. Although Olofsson had to go back to prison to serve the rest of his term, which amounted to almost six years, Kristin and her family would become longtime friends with him and his family.

After their rescue, the hostages reiterated their claims that during the ordeal they were more frightened of the police than of the men who had taken them hostage. They had clearly identified with their captors, and created an alternate reality for themselves.

In the days and months following the rescue, all of the hostages remained loyal to the perpetrators. One hostage even accused the psychiatrists of trying to brainwash them to turn against their captors.[228] When the hostages were finally willing to testify against their captors a full six months after the holdup, Olsson was sentenced to ten years as the instigator of the ordeal.

Bonding with the Perpetrator

The Stockholm Syndrome[229]—this identification of victims with their abusers—has been linked to many famous kidnapping and hostage cases in the United States, including Patty Hearst, Elizabeth Smart, Shawn Hornbeck and Jaycee Dugard. After Dugard's rescue in August of 2009, kidnapping survivor Shawn Hornbeck was asked why he thought she had never escaped. "You're brainwashed," he said. "It's as simple as that. I know people use that term a lot, but that's what happens to you. It's like you are on autopilot, only someone else is controlling all the switches. They control every little, minute detail in your life. Everything."[230]

Others who may experience the Stockholm Syndrome include cult members, concentration camp prisoners or prisoners of war, abused children, incest victims, victims of battering or psychological abuse, and those in intimidating or controlling relationships. Readers who have experienced domestic violence may understand the feelings of the Stockholm Syndrome all too well, since power and control are the hallmarks of abusive relationships.

The human mind and heart are complex. But for the purposes of this book, this story helps us witness the phenomenon of four victims held in a bank vault by robbers whom they had never previously met. In a matter of hours, the victims felt safer and more protected with their captors than the police. Possibly this story can also help us understand why human trafficking victims, some who have been groomed by their captors for months or years, can remain loyal to—and return to—those captors, even when that seemingly makes no sense to an outsider.

The same dynamic that made the hostages in that Stockholm bank feel more trust and loyalty toward the robbers holding them captive than they did toward the police, keeps victims from escaping traffickers who have enslaved them. The Stockholm Syndrome may finally have been identified in 1973, but its effects are nothing new. Harriet Tubman, that courageous and godly woman who believed that, like Moses, she had to lead her people to freedom, once said, "If I could have convinced more slaves that they were slaves, I could have freed thousands more."[231]

How does this kind of brainwashing occur? It usually starts with abuse, a common occurrence in every type of human trafficking case. Captors and/or abusers make a practice of controlling their victims through fear and intimidation, usually starting with verbal abuse. When a girl is soliciting johns on the track (those streets where soliciting is popular) and she hasn't picked up a john in a little while, her pimp will frequently drive up and have her get in the car. "Get out there and make me some money," he screams at her. (That's the PG version.) Then he may tell her that she's worthless and call her names that would not be appropriate to print here. He may threaten her with a beating or other physical abuse.

The threats are all too real. The violence, which impacts 86 percent of U.S. women and girls sold into prostitution according to one survey,[232] varies from slaps and punches to more overt physical force and even hor-rific torture. This physical abuse has a psychological component as well. It encourages victims to cooperate, since they seek to avoid being pun-ished for infractions like bringing home less money than their quota.

It's also not uncommon for perpetrators to punish one victim in front of another to reinforce the fear that they are capable of inflicting severe injury or even death. This extreme physical abuse usually occurs when a victim attempts to resist the captors' control. By making an example of the rebel, even to the point of killing her, they can cement the others' cooperation, which ultimately will enhance their profits despite the loss of an income-generating body.[233]

Beating a slave's friend or co-slave instead of the person who supposedly committed the misdeed is another powerful tool when it comes to controlling victims. Threatening a woman's family is even more effective.

Young girls who are sex trafficked are commonly told by their pimp that he will go get a cherished little sister, cousin or some other young and innocent girl she knows and loves, and force her into prostitution if she doesn't do what he wants. Threats of harm might also be made against the victims' parents, friends or children. The Las Vegas dancer trafficked to Japan in Chapter Five was successfully kept in check for years by regular reminders from her traffickers that they knew where her daughter lived and would have people "take care of her family" if she didn't obey them. To keep her family safe, she did what she was told to do. She knew all too well that her registration form contained all the information they would need to execute their threats.

Getting a girl hooked on drugs, a common tactic in the sex trade, is another way that traffickers gain cooperation and loyalty from their victims. As mentioned in Chapter One, in our small town in central Oregon, there are credible reports of young homeless girls waking up in the middle of the night with needles in their arms. A short time later they disappear from the homeless camp. Rumor has it that they are now with traffickers, who control them completely simply by giving and withholding drugs. Once victims become addicts, they will do anything to get the drugs they crave. As an added incentive, traffickers then hold out a carrot. The more money a victim brings in, the better drugs she or he will be given.

As we saw in the Stockholm bank with Kristin, eventually the lack of control over one's own life creates a strange bonding—and even a sense of safety—with one's captor. That explains why traffickers such as pimps can actually control their victims by threatening to leave them. In addition, captors go to great lengths to convince their victims that no one would want to help them even if they asked. Victims are told that police will not believe the victim, that the police are corrupt, that the trafficker has links to the police, or that the victim is at a legal disadvantage in some way and will be arrested. Eventually, victims come to fear police involvement just as Kristin did and to see their captor as the person who is protecting them from law enforcement or others who might have been able to assist in her escape. Yes, in an effort to survive that's how twisted the mind can become.

It is particularly easy for the trafficker to convince people who are not U.S. citizens that they'll be deported if they try to escape their captivity. For many victims, deportation and the shame of returning to their homeland in this manner could cause the victim to lose such face that they believe staying under the existing slavery is a better option. Others simply fear an outside world and legal system about which they know nothing.

Captors of both foreign-born and U.S. citizens feed this fear and rehearse a script with their victims in case the law does catch up with them. These traffickers know the questions the police will likely ask, and victims are trained to answer in such a way that the perpetrator is not implicated. This scripting, as it's called, is enforced by the other means of control discussed in this chapter, including threats to the victims and their loved ones.

Why Victims Don't Run

There are a host of other reasons—most also symptoms of the Stockholm Syndrome—that explain why human trafficking victims may not try to escape even when the door may be unlocked and the coast clear:

- Victims are hyper vigilant with respect to the captors' needs or beliefs, and identify with the captor's perspective on the world. They experience intense gratefulness for small kindnesses (such as the captor/abuser not administering a beating when expected) because the captor/abuser holds the power of life and death over them. This triggers a sense of dependence and helplessness.

- Most human trafficking victims don't have friends or family nearby. This holds just as true for victims of forced labor as it does for sex-trafficked victims. As we saw in the last chapter, pimps keep the girls on what is called the circuit, moving them from place to place every few weeks. This may be within a city or from city to city. Either way, the motivation is to keep them from setting up alliances with other girls or with johns who could facilitate escape. It also helps keep the victims disoriented. "Where am I?" prostituted individuals commonly ask once they've escaped or been rescued. Not knowing what city, state or even what country they are in adds to the difficulty of leaving.

- One of the telltale signs of human trafficking is that the trafficker often has possession of the victim's identification, driver's license, social security cards, passports, etc. In the Las Vegas dancer's case, the woman who met her at the airport said that Japan was experiencing a lot of trouble with identity theft and advised that the dancer hand over all her documents—including her passport and visa—for safekeeping. Stripping away these tangible forms of identification makes it that much more difficult for victims to leave or to seek assistance.

- Dishonesty feeds on honest people who feel they owe their captor something. People who are in debt bondage—whether picking tomatoes or being sexually trafficked—often feel that they can't leave because of their debt to the very person who's stealing their soul. Since the victim has most often been duped into becoming involved with the trafficker—to say nothing of the fact that the financial charges incurred have been exaggerated—that sense of moral obligation is as misguided as it is immobilizing.

- Even if the victim wants to leave and has the opportunity to escape, the fear of reprisal against their loved ones—or themselves if they are ever found by their captor—may convince them to stay. Victims may know from experience with the captor/abuser that they will be found. And they may believe that if they were found, the consequences would be worse for them than if they had never left. Ultimately, the fear of what could happen if they left can become much greater than the fear of what has happened or is happening to them in captivity. The irony here is that even knowing all of the above, victims may still find a way to deny their captor's true nature in order to shield themselves from their reality.

- Language barriers, cultural differences, and a basic lack of understanding about victims' rights and available services will keep many human trafficking victims from even thinking about trying to flee.

- In addition, most human trafficking victims suffer from Post-Traumatic Stress Disorder (PTSD). According to the American Psychiatric Association, the condition may occur when a person has experienced extreme traumatic stressors involving direct personal experience of an event that involves actual or threatened death or serious injury; threat to one's personal integrity; witnessing an event that involves death, injury or a threat to the physical integrity of another person; learning about unexpected or violent death, serious harm, or threat of death or injury experienced by a family member or other close associate.[234] The symptoms of PTSD can include flashbacks—mentally reliving the horrors they experienced during their life of captivity—as well as the avoidance of stimuli associated with the trauma. Victims of PTSD can also experience difficulty falling or staying asleep, anger, and hyper vigilance. By definition, the symptoms of PTSD can last for years, and they can cause serious problems in social, occupational, or other important areas of everyday life (for example, problems at work and in personal relationships).[235]

Shaking the Syndrome

Fortunately, some human trafficking victims do manage to shake the Stockholm Syndrome and break the chains of human trafficking. Kendall Simmons was a strong student from a good home, whose parents cared about her in all the right ways.[236] But that's not always enough to immunize a young person against the persuasions of the wrong boy. So when Kendall's boyfriend of three months, Darren "DJ" Evans, was kicked out of his mother's home, she moved out of her parents' home and into DJ's car to live with him.

Within days, he entreated her to sell her body. "Baby, we need money," he told her. "Please, baby, do it for me."[237]

She believed she was in love with DJ, so she did what he asked and started walking the strip, turning up to twenty-five tricks a day. She was just sixteen.

Things soon went from bad to worse when DJ began beating her. Each day she headed off to high school wearing sunglasses to hide a black eye or trying to walk without the limp that a beating had induced. As soon as classes were out, she hit the streets to earn money that she was required to bring back to DJ.

Kendall knew that DJ was an alcoholic. She knew he was abusive and controlling. Yet she believed she was in love with him and that he would eventually change his behavior. She believed they would live happily ever after. It took a year for her to decide that she had had enough and that she was ready to go back to her loving family. "I always had a family that I could run back to," she told a reporter. "But I'm rare. I know there's a lot of girls out there that don't have families like mine."[238]

The day after Kendall told DJ she was leaving him for good and actually moved out, he called her at her parents' home and begged to come see her. She agreed. She wanted to show him and herself that she was strong now. The decision nearly cost Kendall her life.

DJ strangled and kicked her, tortured and humiliated her, including requiring her to bark like a dog in order to get a glass of water. Fortunately, she was able to call 911 before he broke her cell phone in half. When the police came, the strangulation marks on her neck were all the evidence they needed to arrest DJ, who subsequently pled guilty to second degree assault and promoting prostitution. Prostitution? At sixteen, Kendall was not a prostitute, but a victim of human trafficking. He was sentenced to eight years in prison.

Kendall proved to be a courageous and determined survivor. With the support of her family, she graduated with her high school class and went on to community college in a nearby town. She's majoring in Criminal Justice and hopes to one day join law enforcement as a detective or an investigator.[239]

Healing after Victimization

As Kendall's and other survivors' families know, rescue is the beginning, not the end of the healing for the victim. There are often lasting mental and physical health issues in addition to the emotional challenges.

Because of the extent of terror and abuse trafficking victims have experienced, there is much work to be done before they can re-enter normal life. This is especially true of sex-trafficking victims whose self-image has been systematically stripped away. Victims have usually been ostracized from their friends and family by their perpetrators and/or as a survival mechanism. Likewise, it is hard for victims to return to normal life because they feel everyone knows what happened to them and are embarrassed and afraid of being exposed.

In addition, victims will often take on their abuser's perspective during captivity as part of the bonding with captors mentioned earlier in this chapter. So in addition to not wanting to leave their traffickers, after a period of time victims may come to share their captors' belief systems. These new beliefs can differ hugely from their previous ones and may include believing that their parents, family, and friends never really loved them like their captor/abuser does or that they cannot survive without their captor/abuser. Victims have been known to threaten their family and friends with restraining orders if they continue to "interfere" or help them escape their situation.

Trapped in the Life

Having been stripped of their self-image to the point of adopting an alien set of values and fearing rejection for what they believe they have now become, some victims of sex trafficking who are rescued won't break free from that kind of life. Since most lack education and job skills, a percentage will inevitably return to the "work" they now believe is their only option instead of remaining in safety.

Breaking free from sex trafficking can be especially difficult for juveniles, virtually all of whom become pimp-controlled. Built of desperation and fear, the bonds they form with their pimps are even more difficult to break. This can be particularly true for the young girl who believes she's in love with the very man who is pimping her out. "The problem is that there is no methadone for a bad relationship," says Rachel Lloyd, a former child sex-worker and the director of Girls Educational and Mentoring Services (GEMS), a program in New York which helps girls escape and stay away from the lives they've led.[240] That helps explain why some girls continue working for pimps even after the pimps are incarcerated.

Giving Help and Shelter

Despite the fact that only the most effective treatment will help even a fraction of the estimated 100,000 child victims[241] reclaim their lives, there are way too few residential treatment centers in the United States for sex-trafficked children. "You can't just take them home," says Ernie Allen, president of the National Center for Missing and Exploited Children. "The challenge is, there are not enough resources."[242]

While social service organizations seem to be developing a better understanding of the specific needs of teens rescued from sex trafficking, putting a victim in a traditional foster home hasn't been the best solution. Children and teens subjected to commercial sexual exploitation have been conditioned by their pimps to escape from a foster home as soon as they get a chance. That can happen as quickly as entering the front door and walking out the back door. These youngsters need special services tailored to address the specific abuses and brainwashing they have experienced while being sex trafficked.

As of the writing of this book, I know of multiple shelters in the works that plan to tackle these specific needs. I pray many more shelters will soon be available and generous with the services and unconditional love that will be imperative when it comes to giving these precious young beings the new start they deserve. These victims are our kids, and they deserve a hand up so they can live their lives to the fullest.

Don't Let Them Get Away with This

Human trafficking and slavery thrive in ignorance, silence and secrecy. But ordinary people like you and me can protest and in a united voice say "No more!" We owe it to the victims as well as ourselves not to turn away, but to speak out instead.

Jacobo Timmerman, who was a political prisoner during the Holocaust says, "The Holocaust will be understood not so much for the number of victims as for the magnitude of silence. And what obsesses me the most is the repetition of silence."[243] We can't let that continue.

When I became aware of the injustices, the horrors, and the atrocities human traffickers and slave masters commit every day, I couldn't keep quiet. And while I don't spend my every waking moment talking to people about human trafficking, I regularly look for opportunities to open people's eyes and help them to understand that these things are happening every day and everywhere—sometimes right under our own noses. I ask you to do the same.

Speak up about modern-day slavery to people you know—your friends, your family members, the leaders in your church or anyone who is willing to listen.

Once a year, there is a Sunday dedicated to anti-human trafficking issues. Freedom Sunday says: *I will not tolerate any Child of God in our neighborhood, in our backyard, in my sphere of influence to be trafficked, to be sold, to be used.* Talk to your church leadership and ask that your church join the movement to stop slavery in this great nation on that Sunday.

Speak to your local law enforcement and social service agencies, to state agencies and to national leaders, including your own congressional representatives and others who can make a big difference.

And when you see ads in publications, make your voice heard and protest vigorously. At the Super Bowl, many sent letters and emails of remonstration not only to the magazine running exploitative sex ads but also to many mainstream corporations that advertised in the magazine. Mainstream companies do not like that kind of spotlight, and will usually pressure the publication in question to change its policies.

All the perpetrator asks is that we remain silent. Take a pledge to break that silence and make as much noise about the atrocity of human trafficking as you can. Because as long as one of us is enslaved, then none of us is truly free.

Discussion Questions for Chapter 7

*Terrors overwhelm me; my dignity is driven away as by the wind,
my safety vanishes like a cloud.*

—JOB 30:15

1. What does the Stockholm Syndrome have to do with modern-day slavery?

2. Discuss a news story where the victim seems to have bonded with his or her captor. Why do you think the victim may not have escaped when it seemed he or she had opportunities?

3. Families and friends of Stockholm Syndrome victims can help by being available to the victim. How might one support a loved one who is trapped, while still respecting his or her boundaries and without endangering him or her?

4. Harriet Tubman said she could have rescued many more slaves if she could have convinced them they were slaves. If she had that dilemma when slavery was named as such, discuss the difficulty a victim experiences today in escaping modern-day slavery.

5. How might you help your church promote awareness about human trafficking?

Chapter 8

Wolves in Sheep's Clothing

Sadly, our pop culture—which is exported around the world—glamorizes the role of the pimp, which promotes sex trafficking.
—MARK LAGON

It's an extreme uphill battle for the trafficking survivor of any age to move past the horrors of captivity—the months or years of terror, abuse, neglect, pain, subjugation, and humiliation—and live normal, healthy, productive lives. The resulting deep, lasting scars might seem beyond healing. But those of us who approach the work of ending this modern-day horror from a Christian standpoint know we serve a God who is big enough to reach out in love and who has the power to heal not only human trafficking's victims, but sometimes its perpetrators as well. For often, they, too, have been victimized.[244]

Hurting People Hurt People

By the time Jason Foster*[245] was in his mid twenties, his father, although it brought him enormous pain, prayed agonizingly for Jason to be removed

139

from this earth because he was hurting so many people with his life choices. The prayers hadn't started out that way. Neither had Jason.

Jason grew up in one of the nicer neighborhoods in Salem, Oregon. His dad, a doctor, and his mom, a stay-at-home mother, were loving parents who strove to provide their two sons with everything they would need to succeed. They also tried to be good neighbors and were active in the community. The couple lived Christian lives to the best of their abilities and loved God with all their hearts. They went to church every Sunday and prayed fervently for their family and especially their kids. In short, they had a good reputation and it was well earned.

Jason was a sweet young boy who got along well with others. In addition, he was smart, strong, athletically gifted and a natural leader. He had it all going for him. There was no reason to question the bright future this young man would have, unless one knew that as a preschooler he had fallen victim to sexual abuse that would change the course of his life.

Jason and his friend Debbie* regularly played out in the forest behind his house, enjoying the simple pleasures of childhood. Childhood dreams that live in a child's mind can transform a simple tree fort into a space ship. The bicycle without training wheels becomes a race car and the baseball hit over the backyard fence becomes the grand slam that wins the World Series.

In Debbie's world, however, life wasn't so simple or so pure. Her parents not only had become involved in pornography, they had involved their little girl. Out of her hurt came Jason's. In the midst of their play, she would insist that Jason go with her to the bathroom to perform the sexual acts that her parents had introduced to her.

Jason never felt comfortable with what happened in that bathroom. "Can't we just hug?" he protested. That is how he had been taught to show affection.

Instead of agreeing, she threatened to tell Jason's parents about what they'd been doing if he didn't agree to participate in their sexual game.

Years later, Jason still doesn't know why he didn't just call the girl's bluff. In hindsight, she certainly had more to lose than he. But he was ashamed and he was scared. So he continued to comply with the abuse, which in his words would become "a cornerstone of the person that I [became]."

By puberty, feelings of guilt about the abuse turned to anger. He thought he could handle his feelings, but they were handling him. "I hadn't told anybody," he says. "I had no intention of ever telling anybody that type of a thing, especially being a boy." When the anger boiled over, he turned violent, hurting himself and others without so much as a second thought.

At age fourteen, Jason began experimenting with drugs and alcohol. He found that alcohol made him "comfortably numb." Since he still hadn't told his parents about what had happened—let alone asked them for help—the attempts to self-medicate helped him get through the day.

When his parents realized that Jason was experiencing more than just normal teenage rebellion, they did everything they could to help. They talked with him and grounded him and took away privileges, trying to provide an even balance of love and discipline with boundaries, but nothing seemed to work. Finally, they sent him to a boarding school where he nearly died of an overdose. The boarding school expelled him and sent him home.

His parents refused to give up on their son. Recognizing that he had a substance abuse problem, they admitted him to the best adolescent recovery program they could find. At sixteen, when most kids were trying to be on their best behavior so their parents would let them get their driver's license, Jason was in his first lock up. He felt hurt, betrayed and even angrier than before.

Rehab did not bring Jason around. Instead, in an attempt to regain the power that had been stripped from him as a child, he careened from doing dangerous drugs to engaging in dangerous activities. He quickly graduated from buying drugs from counter-culture drug dealers to robbing them of their wares. "What could they do?" he reasoned. "Call the cops on me?" Knowing that he had hurt someone else—in essence sharing the misery—helped ease the pain he carried inside. If he was going to feel such hurt all the time, then others should as well.

Ultimately, however, what he really sought was a sense of control. He would find that control at age fifteen, not through healthy avenues, but through a pimp who had chosen to hang out at Jason's school. The pimp was recruiting new girls for his "stable," a term used in trafficking circles for the group of girls a pimp is selling.

At that time, parents sending their kids to what was the newest and arguably nicest high school in Salem, filled with upper middle class students—never dreamed their children could potentially meet a pimp on the premises who would change their lives. But no one seemed to question the presence of this older guy draped in gold jewelry who regularly drove a different, expensive car.

The other kids at school steered clear of Devin*, the pimp. Not Jason. Like a bee to honey, he went straight up to Devin. Before long, the two had become friends. Jason's charisma and charm soon won him favor with the other pimps with whom Devin hung out, and Jason was embraced and accepted into the pimp family. Their lifestyle fascinated him as much as the control they exerted over the girls intrigued and appealed to him. Before long, he didn't just want to witness their way of life, he wanted to share it. Finally, being the one in power could help him forget about what had happened during his childhood.

The pimp family schooled Jason in their ways and soon he turned out his first girl, Claire*, the girl he had been dating. He had painted a picture of the life they would share together, telling her that if she really cared about him, she would do this for him. Eventually she agreed, without even asking how the money would be split. That was fine with Jason. He had no intention of sharing with Claire a dime of the money she earned.

Just as he had planned, Jason began to drop off Claire on "dates," and then pocketed the money she brought back. She would be the first of scores of girls who sold their bodies and lined his pockets with 100 percent of their earnings.

Over the years that followed, Jason's life plummeted into deeper and then deepest destruction. In addition to becoming a full-fledged pimp, he committed crimes involving drugs, weapons and stolen property. It was all part of "the game," as pimping is known, that Jason had chosen as a lifestyle.

For the next fourteen years, in between prison stints, Jason pimped girls on the streets, in car lots and in some of the most famous brothels in Nevada. He lived life as fast and as fearlessly as he could, becoming a renowned rap artist in the process. But even after many years, he still hadn't found that high that he was seeking. No matter what he did— pimping girls, enjoying their earnings, rapping and cutting albums, and becoming known in the underworld as the notorious young white guy who had excelled in pimping and rapping—he felt increasingly empty and unhappy.

He was leading a life of desperation and he knew it. On two separate occasions when he felt he had hit bottom, Jason called his parents in tears. Each of those points of despair brought him a little closer to getting out of the low life to which he had sunk. He knew what he needed to do, starting with getting away from the booze he knew was killing him. He just couldn't do it alone.

At last, he prayed to Jesus. He was powerless to quit drinking, he admitted as he prayed, and needed help. The next day, despite having consumed copious amounts of alcohol, he awoke feeling fresher than he had in years. He took it as a sign that God was with him. In that instant, he gave up alcohol. He has remained alcohol-free to this day.

But not using alcohol didn't negate the rest of his life, which in addition to pimping included selling and using drugs. Yet God's voice and persistence was clear and steadfast. No matter how far and hard Jason ran after the life of crime and hurting himself and others, God continued to knock on the door of Jason's heart and continued to prove to be the God who still cared for him.

Even so, it would take another year before Jason would relinquish his horrific existence. Finally, after one particularly harrowing experience, he did what he had done several times during his destructive and disastrous life of crime. He went back to his one place of stability and security—to his parents who had never quit praying for him and never quit believing in him even though they had never condoned his sordid lifestyle. Despite the anguish he had caused them, they welcomed their son with open arms, an act that still humbles him.

A Life Reclaimed

Although Jason's struggle to get his life back on track would be studded with pain, he had finally made the decision to live for Christ, no matter the cost. From that day forward, he never returned to the life of crime and destruction.

Jason now speaks to groups of young people, as well as to individuals of all ages. Having seen a lot of perpetrators in my life and very few who have really turned their lives around, I am a major league skeptic when it comes to believing in real-life change for one who has devastated so many lives. However, I can testify to Jason's about-face. Today, Jason is my friend. He is happily married, a father and a man with no scent of religiosity even though he radiates the love of Christ and the gentle love of amazing grace. I can truly vouch for the fact that his is a transformed life.

Answered Prayers

So what is the difference between Jason and so many others whose lives never change? One can never really know the full answer to that question. However, I'm convinced that prayer was one part of the equation. Jason's parents—who continued to love him unconditionally even though they never condoned, accepted or tolerated the havoc he wreaked in so many lives—prayed for him without stopping. They asked their many friends (myself included) and family to pray for him over the years as well. And

God did not ignore those prayers. "The restoration God has done in my life is unquestionably nothing short of a miracle in and of itself," Jason writes in his book, which he hopes to publish.[246]

There's Nothing Cool about Pimps

Jason chose his misguided, destructive path because it provided him with the three things he thought might ease his pain: money, power and respect.

Popular culture in the U.S. doesn't just condone pimping, it often glamorizes it. In feature movies, on TV, and in the world of hardcore hip hop music, pimping is often presented as a thrilling line of "work" to which young men should proudly aspire. One 2005 hardcore hip hop song titled "It's Hard Out Here for a Pimp," which chronicles the some-times violent struggles of a street pimp to make a living off his "bitches" and "hos," won an Academy Award for best song.[247]

In too many neighborhoods, pimps are looked up to as symbols of success. Why not? They have all the trappings that money can buy and their jobs are even celebrated. And not just by the entertainment indus-try. In a large number of cities, including our own small town, "Pimp and Ho" parties are publically advertised and held at local nightclubs.

Excuse me?

There is nothing at all glamorous or socially acceptable about pimps or pimping. Real-life pimps are among the worst kind of predators our culture has to offer, and they are a very real danger to young women and girls in America today. They are criminals who recruit, coerce, and threaten our young women and girls, and then sell them into prostitu-tion. They traffic their victims from brothel to brothel and from town to town, making it extremely difficult, sometimes impossible, for law enforcement or the victims' families to locate them.

Despite their abysmal record, in modern speech—especially among the young—we elevate pimps by using the word *pimp* in a positive context. "Wow! You're pimped out today!" is said to indicate that some-one is extremely well dressed. What a way to refer to what was once known as our Sunday best. And what a crime. Common sense tells us that the word *pimp* should at best indicate something ugly and vulgar. Instead, on every episode of the popular MTV (Music Television) pro-gram "Pimp My Ride," technicians, body and paint specialists, and artists convert people's beat up, barely-running wrecks into "pimped-out" auto-mobiles anyone would drive down the street with pride.[248]

Since I have become involved in the movement to stop human trafficking, I have come to see the ugliness of the word *pimp* and all it implies. And although I'm not easily offended, I do take offense at its casual use. Using the word *pimp* in the ways I've listed above—and in other ways—not only breaks down moral and social barriers to pimping and sex trafficking, it disguises the true ugliness of what real-life pimps do. Its casual use also dehumanizes the women and young girls who fall victim to pimps and puts a glamorous face on the ugliness. It is human trafficking. It is modern-day slavery.

We've got to debunk this word so that children understand that a pimp isn't the ultimate superstar, but rather a criminal who rapes, beats, uses, and destroys lives. If somebody were to tell me, "Wow! You're really pimped out today!" I would answer, "No, I'm not. I haven't raped any-body and no, I haven't beaten anybody. I haven't kept anybody impris-oned, and I haven't coerced anyone to do the most degrading thing in the world for my own personal profit. No, I'm not pimped out."

Pimps are sometimes considered the worst kind of human traffickers because they use their victims over and over again until they're traded or discarded, or, since few manage to escape, until they die. Sadly, though I've been using the word *pimp* to refer to traffickers in the sex trade, there are a variety of pimps out there. I see little difference between someone profiting off of human slave labor in a factory, a home, a field or a brothel. They're all selling humans, so they're all slaveholders. I don't know anyone who wants to celebrate that.

Identifying Human Traffickers in Your Backyard

A reality check in terms of semantics is just the start of what's needed. We must be willing to expose any pimps—any human traffickers—who all too often operate in our very own communities posing as upstanding community members.

Human traffickers could be people who are considered virtuous members of your church. Think about Given's story in Chapter Two and Pastor Keith who recruited him and others from Zambia. Is there a worse form of usury than to use God's name to abuse others? In my opinion, compelling one to sing God's praises to the point of utter exhaustion is about as low as one can get.

Human traffickers could be respectable local businessmen who own secret sweatshops. Remember Quyen Truong? Kil Soo Lee, the man who held her and hundreds of others in his American Samoa factory where he forced them to sew garments, did business with some of this country's top retail clothing brands.

Human traffickers could be restaurateurs in your hometown. How many people enjoyed a meal at the family chain where Charito worked without having a clue that she and the other Asians were being so mistreated?

Human traffickers could be your neighbors, no matter the income level in which you live. Shyima is only one of an untold number of household slaves being held in this country. A 2004 report concludes "the second highest incidence of forced labor takes place in domestic service in U.S. homes."[249] And that doesn't even count the countless sex slaves squirreled away in brothels discretely run out of ordinary homes in perfectly ordinary neighborhoods.

These human traffickers—these low-down disgusting pimps—excel at three things: manipulation, power and control. They're well versed in the classic brainwashing techniques they use, and take pride in being able to bend other people to their will. A former pimp I interviewed explained that pimps are "at the top of the food chain" because instead of selling dope and setting yourself up to get busted or killed, "you control [your girls] with your mind and get the money without doing anything. You put them at risk and you don't put yourself at risk with jail, all the stuff that can go wrong in that lifestyle."[250]

The pimp world has changed since my source got out of the life of crime, and not for the better. Hard to believe, but life has gotten worse for pimps' victims. "In the old days, the pimps were older men, pimping the girls was called 'the game,' and part of 'the game' was learning a girl's weakness, then manipulating that girl's weakness to get her to go off and do things that's going to benefit you," says the Gulf Coast Coalition Against Human Trafficking's Brad Dennis. "That's 'the game,' that's mind control. But...young guys in this game...don't understand that. They don't understand how to...manipulate [a] girl to do the things that they want her to do. So they resort to nothing but brute force."[251]

Alas, these thugs are now the name of the game. "What we are seeing is younger and younger pimps out there on the tracks," Brad told me. "You go to Atlanta and you see eighteen-, nineteen-, twenty-, twenty-one-year-old pimps, traffickers, with two, three and four girls that they are working. If I'm not an athlete, and I come from a really bad neighborhood, I have two choices after that. I can go into selling drugs or pimping girls."[252] That makes sense in a sick way, since both are seen as glamorous.

Our challenge lies in changing attitudes so that someone who pimps girls is seen as the slave-master he is rather than someone who's cool. Once that happens, then maybe we can begin to stem some of this flow. But we also have to spread the word so that human trafficking targets are more informed and less vulnerable.

Ironically, there are hardly any human trafficking victims who haven't consented to go with the trafficker. Of course, they're not told the truth. Instead, the trafficker says something like, "Come to America. You'll work in a restaurant and make twenty dollars a day in tips." Though that's huge money to a lot of people, the victim can easily verify that even busboys can earn those kinds of tips in the U.S. What they don't realize is that when they get here, instead of waiting tables in that restaurant, they may be dancing a strip pole and turning tricks in a room on the side, with the money going to the perpetrator who trafficks them.

That's one of the real differences between slavery in the old days and modern-day slavery. Historically, slaves were captured. Today, most slaves have consented to work for their traffickers. They've just consented to something very different than what they end up in, so they've been duped by someone smart enough, charming enough, and narcissistic enough to pull off a continued series of hoaxes that destroy people's lives. And because the perpetrators lack compassion and see life as being all about them, there's no reason not to lie if it makes them money. In their mind it seems there's no reason not to hurt somebody as long as it benefits them.

The bottom line is that a perpetrator is a perpetrator is a perpetrator, whether he's trafficking slaves for farm work, domestic work, sex or anything else. Perpetrators do what they do because they profit from it financially and egotistically. It doesn't matter to them that the profit comes at the expense of another.

Those very few with even a shred of conscience do everything they can to expunge that sense of right and wrong. When Jason Foster devastated his girlfriend Claire's life, followed by the lives of so many others, by "turning them out," he refused to let himself consider why a girl would "go sell her body, do the most extreme thing in the world and give you all the money and stay with you." He advised a younger pimp he'd taken under his wing to never even consider why someone would be willing to do that. "If you sit here and try to ponder that and think about it, you will go crazy because there is absolutely no sane reason," he told him.[253] In short, he knew what he was doing was immoral. At the time, however, that just didn't matter.

For traffickers, the human cost to their victims isn't even a consideration. The sex slaves, the factory and farm workers, the domestic or restaurant workers are simply a tool to make the perpetrator money—and in the process to make them look important. To a perpetrator, using a victim is as casual and calculated as a construction worker picking up a hammer.

So how do you recognize a human trafficker? You can't tell just by looking, the same way you can't tell whether someone batters his spouse just by looking at him. How do you recognize abusers? Because they abuse. How do you recognize traffickers? Because they traffic. And just as there's nothing glamorous about the guy who beats his wife or girlfriend, there's nothing glamorous about a pimp or any other kind of human trafficker.

But that doesn't mean that there isn't hope for some of these people, no matter how far they've fallen. As we saw in Jason's story, people are a product of who they were created to be and the circumstances that they have lived through. But with God's intervention and their own deep desire to reform, they can be redeemed.

Never Forget to Pray

Sometimes, we do everything we can do to "help" God. Some of us are "good" at that. But when we hit the end of our abilities, we realize that all we have left to do is pray. In reality, that's the first thing we should do.

For many years, I have followed news stories and prayed for the people involved. I do believe that our prayers always make a difference. "The prayer of a righteous person is powerful and effective."[254]

During a trip to India in 2008, my heart was drawn to a dear young teen and trafficking survivor by the name of Sunita. I was able to leave some funds to help her in her endeavor to support herself by becoming a tailor. Beyond that, however, there was nothing I could tangibly do for her. Since that time, I have prayed for her often. I believe those prayers will change the course of her life. As I've received reports about Sunita, my belief in prayer is confirmed. God hears and answers prayers.

So how should we pray for human trafficking situations? The first step is to take the time to pray. As we pray, listening to the Holy Spirit within us, the Lord gives us more to pray about and, I believe, gives us the prayers that God wants prayed.

So what does the Holy Spirit sound like? Someone once said that the Holy Spirit feels like a "hunch" inside us. It's as we begin to listen to that still, small inner voice (or hunch) in our hearts that we learn to recognize the voice of the Holy Spirit. As we listen and pray, and listen and pray, that love relationship between us—God's children—and the Lord develops. And that enables us to be more and more "spot on" in our prayers for others, including human trafficking victims, survivors, and perpetrators.

Prayer *does* change things. Even Jesus prayed, and still does pray for us.[255] Let's join Jesus in praying that slavery be stopped in our lifetime.

Discussion Questions for Chapter 8

He lies in wait like a lion in cover;
he lies in wait to catch the helpless;
he catches the helpless and drags them off in his net.

—PSALM 10:9

1. Has your view of the life of a pimp changed since reading this book? If so, how? How might those changes be reflected in your life?

2. Pimps are not the only types of perpetrators of human trafficking. Discuss several types of traffickers and how they might be similar or different.

3. If Jason Foster could be redeemed, certainly God affords that chance to everyone. Many, however, never change. Discuss why prayer was the key to Jason's redemption and how prayer may be similarly implemented in your community.

4. Money and power seem to be the most common motivators for traffickers. How can we use the power of our spending to help stop modern-day slavery?

5. Locate a news story about a trafficker and discuss what might have been his or her motivation for the crime, and how we as Christians might make trafficking more difficult for the traffickers?

Chapter 9

On the Front Lines of Modern-Day Slavery

Love begins at home, and it is not how much we do...
but how much love we put in that action.

—MOTHER TERESA

The problem of human trafficking can seem as overwhelming as it is grim. But there are those who are working to change this situation. For starters, church people like Brad Dennis, who travels to the Super Bowl every year to rescue human trafficking victims, are making a remarkable difference. Brad is one of my heroes. In addition to being a devoted Christian, husband and father, and pastoring a small church in Pensacola Florida, he devotes his life to finding missing children and to stopping human trafficking, especially when it involves children.

James 1:27 tells us: *Religion that God our Father accepts as pure and faultless is this: to look after orphans and widows in their distress and to keep oneself from being polluted by the world.* When I walked through the side door of Brad's church, I witnessed that in action. I saw Brad's wife Tammy in the kitchen preparing food for those who hadn't had a good meal for some time. I saw Brad compassionately listening to and directing those whose lives had been shattered by the ruthlessness of human trafficking and drugs. I saw their daughters helping out with computer research for the family's next outreach. These are selfless people who know how to give to others, not for their own glory, but for "pure religion" in order to care for those who without help, cannot care for themselves.

Somehow the words, the action, and the Spirit in Brad's church felt right. It seemed like this is what God intended in Isaiah 61:

> [1] *The Spirit of the Sovereign LORD is on me,*
> *because the LORD has anointed me*
> *to proclaim good news to the poor.*
> *He has sent me to bind up the brokenhearted,*
> *to proclaim freedom for the captives*
> *and release from darkness for the prisoners*
> [2] *to proclaim the year of the Lord's favor*
> *and the day of vengeance of our God,*
> *to comfort all who mourn,*
> [3] *and provide for those who grieve in Zion—*
> *to bestow on them a crown of beauty*
> *instead of ashes,*
> *the oil of joy*
> *instead of mourning,*
> *and a garment of praise*
> *instead of a spirit of despair.*
> *They will be called mighty oaks,*
> *a planting of the LORD*
> *for the display of his splendor.*

Brad and his family believe not only in God but in people. They are willing to go the second, third, and seventh (the number of perfection) mile to walk alongside those who have been harmed by the fallen nature of humankind and the byproducts of that fallen nature.

While many churches are consumed with building projects and church growth programs, Brad serves. In Matthew 23:11, Jesus said the greatest among us will be the servant. Brad's life exemplifies that. His phone rings constantly with requests for shoes, coats, baby formula and rent. The calls that cost him the most in time, money and heart are those reporting a missing child.

One of those children was a sixteen-year-old from his hometown named Shauna Newell, [256] who had been recruited by a "bottom girl" attending her high school. After much protest, Shauna finally talked her mother into letting her go to her new friend's house after school. Shauna asked for a glass of water and that's the last thing she remembered for a couple of days. When she awoke in a daze, she was being raped by one of the five guys who had paid for the 'privilege' over the span of a few days.

Meanwhile, Shauna's family and friends who had been frantically searching for her called in reinforcements. Dennis is known in that community to be proactive and willing to get out there. In fact, his position as director of Search Operations for the KlaasKids Foundation resulted from the months Brad spent helping to look for Marc Klaas' daughter Polly. Brad is not afraid of getting his hands dirty, and works alongside others for the greater good. So he and his search team went to work trying to find and rescue Shauna.

In my interview with Shauna, she credits Brad with the communication that set her free. "Brad Dennis and the KlaasKids Foundation were on their tail and got the message out to them that 'this is where we're looking for her and if she just so happens to show up in this area, then it'd save you a lot of trouble.'"

The traffickers dropped Shauna off at a convenience store. "I got out of the car and I ran, and just ran and ran and ran," she says. "I was so scared I was just running. I was completely pale, my hair was all matted up, I had blood all over the place, two black eyes, had bite marks all over my body. When my mom saw me, she almost didn't even recognize me. My mom said it just didn't look like me. She said she looked at my eyes and it didn't even look like I was there any more."[257]

In the blood tests administered after Shauna was flown to the hospital, doctors found traces of multiple drugs that the traffickers had given her. She had been in a drug-induced state the entire time of her captivity.

Among other things, they also discovered and treated Shauna for internal injuries sustained during the repeated rapes.

Regrettably, the traffickers were never prosecuted in Shauna's case. But at least she was rescued and is able to live a life of freedom, recovering from the horrendous experience of having been trafficked.

That's what drives Brad to the streets to provide comfort to those in need. He brings along everything from packets of toiletries to the right-sized shoes he's managed to find for someone whose footwear was giving out or gone. And he relentlessly searches for human trafficking victims.

When Brad isn't preparing his message for church services, he's out doing what it says in Isaiah 61:1–2. He's serving where he's needed. In 2008, when Brad's congregation was seeking a service project, rather than looking for a high profile project, Brad went where no one was watching and began serving in low-income state housing, which rented units daily and weekly.

The purpose behind choosing that venue was clear. These were the people who were considered so poor and low-life that no one else was interested in being there. Brad also knew these folks were prime targets for human trafficking. It wasn't long before he encountered a situation where someone was selling a baby. Authorities were notified and today the baby is safe.

Walking through that complex with Brad is like walking through the villages in India with Mother Teresa. Pure love, love that cares for the orphans and children, is hard to resist. As a pastor, as well as a defender of the weak and those whose lives have been damaged by the modern-day atrocity of human trafficking, Brad is one of those people we can look up to and want to emulate. He simply says, "The body of Christ is made for things like this, and I count it a privilege to be a fellow soldier among so many passionate and wonderful believers."[258]

~

Brad is just one of thousands of Christians making a difference. "The church and people of faith as a whole have historically served as powerful agents of change," says former Ambassador-at-Large and Director of the Office to Monitor and Combat Trafficking in Persons (TIP) Mark Lagon, who also served as Executive Director and CEO of the Polaris Project. "The faith-based community moves beyond advocacy and policy—critical components—and on to protective care, support and ultimately healing. We have seen faith communities fill a desperate need when it comes to victim identification. They are often the first line of defense, encountering victims long before traditional law enforcement or even social service providers."[259]

Of course we don't live just within a Christian world, we live in the real world. And there are plenty of people who aren't churchgoers, or who may be churchgoers but who operate in another arena, who are also doing tremendous things. In law enforcement one of those stars is Keith Bickford.

Keith is a big guy with a big heart. He's a Multnomah County Deputy Sheriff and a Deputized Special U.S. Marshall who currently serves as the Director of the Oregon Human Trafficking Task Force charged with investigating and prosecuting cases of human trafficking throughout the State of Oregon. He's also the founder and leader of Oregonians Against Trafficking Humans, the same organization for which I lead the central Oregon contingency.

However, there's more to the man than his credentials. Some people do their job and do it well. Bickford certainly does his best to prosecute human traffickers to the fullest extent of the law. But he goes beyond that. He cares so deeply about stopping human trafficking that it's as though his heart beats to do the work. He does everything within his power and within the law to rescue its victims and see to it that they receive services to which they're entitled.

When I asked him about his greatest victories, he pointed to a case where a victim was freed from the horrific farm labor slavery in which he was trapped. He received the surgeries, follow-up medical care, and counseling he needed to recover from the damage his captors had done to him. The perpetrators, however, were never charged or convicted. "To me, that doesn't seem like a very big win," Bickford says. "But every time I see the victim, he thanks me for saving his life, so I guess that's okay. I'll take it."[260]

Bickford not only helps human trafficking victims directly, he helps them by sharing his expertise with other agencies. When our first trafficking victim was brought to us in Bend, Oregon, we contacted Bickford. He gave us numbers to call for services to help her, tips about pitfalls we might encounter in the process, and the correct connections for law enforcement and legal counsel. In short, he patiently and carefully walked us through every step along the way. Each day when I called, he inquired about how the victim we were helping was doing. Even though he had never met her, he obviously cared about her as a person.

Bickford doesn't just devote his energies to fighting trafficking one perpetrator—or one victim—at a time. He also trains and engages law enforcement and community agencies, and has done a tremendous amount of work to help make the dream of more shelter beds for under-age, sex-trafficking victims available. I've often said that Bickford's biggest risk is that his heart is as big as all outdoors. I pray for him often. He is a man whose life is like a rock dropping in the water, with all the ripples responsible for many saved lives and many new forces engaged in the fight against human trafficking.

But we can't rely on law enforcement, government or even our churches to solve this. In the end, it's up to each of us to challenge this heinous crime taking place in our backyards. That's not always easy.

Protecting Communities against Slavery

In November 2008, during my trip to India, I discovered that some villages that had been completely enslaved prior to the intervention of non-governmental organizations (NGOs) had not only been freed, but had actually been effectively protected against future trafficking. In this village-by-village anti-slavery operation, first the schools are formed and children educated. Then anti-slavery activists begin to work with the women in the community, followed by the men. Once the women and men are on board—with new understanding about what slavery is and that citizens have rights, and possibly even recognizing they had been enslaved—the villagers begin to come together as a community. They have meetings to discuss slavery, as well as what to do if the traffickers come and how to protect one another from trafficking.

At some point, the village becomes immune to human trafficking. The community awareness and determination to keep slavery out makes it undesirable for traffickers, especially since the chances of them succeeding in their criminal activities is as low as the chances of prosecution are high. So, as one local said, the traffickers don't come there anymore.

We can wage a similar campaign here in America. The community where I live has organized and the entire area is becoming aware. Once people realize that slavery exists here in the United States and that it's in our communities, I find that people *want* to be on board. They want to help fight slavery. So the tips about possible trafficking activities begin to flow in. Law enforcement officers then follow up on those reports once they, too, become aware, and work to stop this crime.

Admittedly, it's a very uncomfortable self-assessment as we begin to understand our part in this—how we unknowingly participate or react when we see human trafficking. It's more comfortable to try and keep that "slavery dust" from getting on us instead of getting involved, says Lou de Baca, U.S. Ambassador-at-Large, Office to Monitor and Combat Trafficking in Persons (TIP).[261] But if we all link arms, putting aside different political parties, or religious beliefs and join together in the shared hope of stopping modern-day slavery in our lifetime, we can win this tremendously important fight.

The fight to free some 27 million people living in slavery[262]—from nearly every nation and territory on earth—seems like a truly impossible task. Even the notion of freeing the hundreds of thousands of trafficked individuals in this country seems unattainable. But that's not the way Jesus thought. He actually taught His disciples how to approach what seemed like humanly impossible tasks: "Truly I tell you, if you have faith as small as a mustard seed, you can say to this mountain, 'Move from here to there,' and it will move. Nothing will be impossible for you."[263]

Nothing will be impossible for you.

That is a precious promise, one I cling to daily as I pray and do my part to help end human trafficking for good. I am well aware of the many obstacles we will face in this quest. But I also know that my God transcends human possibility, and as incredibly huge and horrible and unjust as global human trafficking and slavery are, God is bigger…and infinitely good and just. That, friends, is how I know that this mountain will one day be moved.

Discussion Questions for Chapter 9

Religion that God our Father accepts as pure and faultless is this:
to look after orphans and widows in their distress and to keep oneself
from being polluted by the world.

—JAMES 1:27

1. How has this book changed your understanding of human trafficking or modern-day slavery in the United States?

2. Is there some way you think you might be able to help stop slavery in our world today?

3. In reading about some of the ways other Christians have worked to stop slavery, have you been inspired? If so, how?

4. If what you've learned about human trafficking has been valuable to you, can you identify a friend to whom you might recommend this book?

Red Flags and Potential Indicators of Human Trafficking [264]

Are you or someone you know being trafficked? Is trafficking happening in your community? Is the situation you encountered human trafficking? The following is a list of potential red flags and indicators of human trafficking.

If you see any of these red flags, call the National Human Trafficking Resource Center hotline at 1-888-3737-888 now to report the situation.

Common Work and Living Conditions
The Individual(s) in Question:

- Is not free to leave or come and go as he/she wishes
- Is under 18 and is providing commercial sex acts
- Is in the commercial sex industry and has a pimp/manager
- Is unpaid, paid very little, or paid only through tips
- Works excessively long and/or unusual hours
- Is not allowed breaks or suffers under unusual restrictions at work
- Owes a large debt and is unable to pay it off
- Was recruited through false promises concerning the nature and conditions of his/her work
- High security measures exist in the work and/or living locations (e.g. opaque windows, boarded up windows, bars on windows, barbed wire, security cameras, etc.)

Poor Mental Health or Abnormal Behavior

- Is fearful, anxious, depressed, submissive, tense, or nervous/paranoid behavior
- Exhibits unusually fearful or anxious behavior after bringing up "law enforcement"
- Avoids eye contact

Poor Physical Health

- Lacks health care
- Appears malnourished
- Shows signs of physical and/or sexual abuse, physical restraint, confinement, or torture

Lack of Control

- Has few or no personal possessions
- Is not in control of his/her own money, no financial records, or bank account
- Is not in control of his/her own identification documents (ID or passport)
- Is not allowed or able to speak for themselves (a third party may insist on being present and/or translating)

Other

- Claims of "just visiting" and inability to clarify where he/she is staying/address
- Lack of knowledge of whereabouts and/or do not know what city he/she is in
- Loss of sense of time
- Has numerous inconsistencies in his/her story

Note: This list is not exhaustive and rather represents a selection of possible indicators. Also, the red flags in this list may not be present in all trafficking cases and are not cumulative.

Notes

1 Matthew 25:40 (Today's New International Version).
2 Written Testimony of Ernie Allen, President and Chief Executive Officer, National Center for Missing and Exploited Children for the U.S. House of Representatives Subcommittee on Crime, Terrorism and Homeland Security Committee on the Judiciary on 'Domestic Minor Sex Trafficking', Washington DC, September 15, 2010. http://www.missingkids.com/missingkids/servlet/NewsEventServlet?LanguageCountry=en_US&PageId=4339
3 "Teen Girls' Stories of Sex Trafficking in U.S." ABC Primetime, February 9, 2006. http://abcnews.go.com/Primetime/story?id=1596778&page=1
4 Kevin Bales. *Disposable People*. University of California Press, Berkeley and Los Angeles, 1999, p. 8.
5 http://www.polarisproject.org/
6 Victims of Trafficking and Violence Protection Act of 2000: Trafficking in Persons Report. U.S. Department of State, 2005. http://www.state.gov/documents/organization/47255.pdf
7 "Assessment of U.S. Activities to Combat Trafficking in Persons 2004." June 2004. http://www.justice.gov/archive/ag/annualreports/tr2004/us_assessment_2004.pdf
8 "Teen Girls' Stories of Sex Trafficking in the US." ABC Primetime, February 9, 2006.
9 R.J. Estes and N.A. Weiner. "The Commercial Sexual Exploitation of Children in the U.S., Canada and Mexico." University of Pennsylvania, Philadelphia: PA, 2001. http://www.sp2.upenn.edu/restes/CSEC_Files/Abstract_010918.pdf
10 "2006 Trafficking in Persons Report." U.S. Department of State, June 2006. http://www.state.gov/documents/organization/34158.pdf
11 http://www.justice.gov/crt/crim/smuggling_trafficking_facts.pdf
12 http://www.missingkids.com/missingkids/servlet/NewsEventServlet?LanguageCountry=en_US&PageId=1321

13 Interview with author, February 3, 2009.

14 Written Testimony of Ernie Allen, President & Chief Executive Officer, National Center for Missing & Exploited Children for the U.S. House of Representatives Subcommittee on Crime, Terrorism and Homeland Security Committee on the Judiciary on 'Domestic Minor Sex Trafficking', Washington DC , September 15, 2010. http://www.missingkids.com/missingkids/servlet/NewsEventServlet?LanguageCountry=en_US&PageId=4339

15 Ibid.

16 National Coalition Against Domestic Violence. "Human Trafficking Facts." http://www.ncadv.org/files/HumanTrafficking.pdf

17 Kevin Bales and Ron Soodalter. *The Slave Next Door.* University of California Press, Berkeley and Los Angeles, CA, 2009, p. 6.

18 Anonymous interview with author.

19 *Human Trafficking*, TV, 2005.

20 Anonymous interview with author.

21 Claire Cain Miller. "Is Blocking Sex Ads a Ploy in Fight Over Free Speech?" *New York Times*, September 6, 2010. http://www.nytimes.com/2010/09/06/technology/06craigslist.html?pagewanted=all

22 This and other documents are available at www.LittleAfrica.com/slaves

23 Martin Barillas. "Report Released on Sexual Exploitation of Children." September 21, 2007. http://www.dailyestimate.com/article.asp?id=11140

24 2 Corinthians 9:7 (Today's New International Version).

25 Compiled from interviews with and emails to author.

26 Dunbar Rowland. *Jefferson Davis, Constitutionalist: His Letters, Papers and Speeches.* J. J. Little & Ives Company, 1923, p. 286.

27 http://freelawanswer.com/law/662-law-3.html

28 Global Forum on Human Trafficking, attended by the author, Carlsbad, CA, October 8, 2009.

29 Luke 10:25-37 (Today's New International Version).

30 John 4:18 (Today's New International Version).

31 John 4:21 (Today's New International Version).

32 http://www.pbs.org/wgbh/aia/part4/4p1535.html

33 Sarah H. Bradford. *Harriet: The Moses of Her People.* Academic Affairs Library, UNC-CH, 1995. http://docsouth.unc.edu/neh/harriet/harriet.html

34 http://www.freemaninstitute.com/Tubman.htm

35 http://www.christianhistorytimeline.com/GLIMPSEF/Glimpses/glmps130.shtml

36 Ibid.

37 Ibid.

38 http://www.pbs.org/wgbh/aia/part4/4p1535.html

39   http://www.christianhistorytimeline.com/GLIMPSEF/Glimpses/
     glmps130.shtml
40   Sarah H. Bradford. *Harriet: The Moses of Her People.* Academic Affairs
     Library, UNC-CH, 1995. http://docsouth.unc.edu/neh/harriet/harriet.
     html
41   Ibid.
42   http://www.lkwdpl.org/wihohio/tubm-har.htm
43   James 2:25 (Today's New International Version).
44   John 4 (Today's New International Version).
45   Malia Zimmerman. "Celebrating Freedom: Justice Finally Achieved for
     Victims of Human Trafficking in American-Samoa Garment Factory
     Case." July 3, 2005. http://www.vps.org/namcali/gala2005/news_
     celebratingfreedom.html
46   Debra Barayuga. "Victims Call Factory 'Slavery'." *Honolulu Star-Bulletin
     News*, July 3, 2005. http://archives.starbulletin.com/2005/07/03/news/
     story1.html
47   Malia Zimmerman. "Celebrating Freedom: Justice Finally Achieved for
     Victims of Human Trafficking in American-Samoa Garment Factory
     Case." July 3, 2005.
48   Debra Barayuga. "Victims Call Factory 'Slavery'." *Honolulu Star-Bulletin
     News*, July 3, 2005. http://archives.starbulletin.com/2005/07/03/news/
     story1.html
49   "Slave Wages-From the Saturday, January 27, 2007 Wall Street Journal."
     Hawaii Reporter, December 22, 2010. http://www.hawaiireporter.
     com/slave-wages-from-the-saturday-january-27-2007-wall-street-journal
50   "Made in the U.S.A.?" National Labor Committee, February 13, 2001.
     http://www.nlcnet.org/reports?id=0215
51   Malia Zimmerman. "Celebrating Freedom: Justice Finally Achieved for
     Victims of Human Trafficking in American-Samoa Garment Factory
     Case." July 3, 2005, http://www.vps.org/namcali/gala2005/news_
     celebratingfreedom.html
52   Ibid.
53   Debra Barayuga. "Victims Call Factory 'Slavery'." *Honolulu Star-Bulletin
     News*, July 3, 2005. http://archives.starbulletin.com/2005/07/03/news/
     story1.html
54   http://cases.justia.com/us-court-of-appeals/F3/472/638/473342/
55   "Anatomy of an International Human Trafficking Case, Pt. 1." http://
     www.fbi.gov/news/stories/2004/july/kilsoolee_071604
56   "Women and Sweatshops." http://www.webster.edu/~woolflm/sweatshops.
     html
57   Ibid.
58   Debra Barayuga. "Victims Call Factory 'Slavery'." *Honolulu Star-Bulletin*

News, July 3, 2005. http://archives.starbulletin.com/2005/07/03/news/story1.html

59 Ibid.

60 http://www.ait.org.tw/infousa/enus/government/forpolicy/docs/ijge0603.pdf

61 Anatomy of an International Human Trafficking Case, Pt. 1." http://www.fbi.gov/news/stories/2004/july/kilsoolee_071604

62 "Made in the USA?" The National Labor Committee, February 13, 2001. http://www.nlcnet.org/reports?id=0215

63 Debra Barayuga. "Victims Call Factory 'Slavery'." *Honolulu Star-Bulletin News*, July 3, 2005. http://archives.starbulletin.com/2005/07/03/news/story1.html

64 Anatomy of an International Human Trafficking Case, Pt. 1." http://www.fbi.gov/news/stories/2004/july/kilsoolee_071604

65 *US v. Kil Soo Lee*, No. 05-10478, (Ninth Circuit, On Appeal from District of Hawaii). http://www.justice.gov/crt/briefs/lee.pdf

66 "Garment Factory Owner Sentenced to 40 Years for Human Trafficking--Dept. of Justice." Department of Justice, June 23, 2005. http://www.nlcnet.org/newsroom?id=0227

67 Ramin Pejan. "Laogai: 'Reform through Labor' in China." *Human Rights Brief: A Legal Resource for the International Human Rights Community 7*, no. 2, 2000. http://www.wcl.american.edu/hrbrief/v7i2/laogai.htm

68 Ibid.

69 Kate McGeown. "China's Christians Suffer for Their Faith." BBC News, November 9, 2004. http://news.bbc.co.uk/2/hi/asia-pacific/3993857.stm

70 Ramin Pejan, "Laogai: 'Reform through Labor' in China." Human Rights Brief: A Legal Resource for the International Human Rights Community 7, no. 2, 2000, p. 22. http://www.wcl.american.edu/hrbrief/07/2laogai.cfm

71 David Batstone, *Not For Sale,* HarperCollins Publishers, New York, NY, 2007, p. 237.

72 Kevin Bales and Ron Soodalter. *The Slave Next Door.* University of California Press, Berkeley and Los Angeles, CA, 2009, p. 51.

73 Ronnie Greene. "A Crop of Abuse." *Miami Herald*, September 1, 2003. http://www.miamiherald.com/2003/09/01/56983/a-crop-of-abuse.html

74 Kevin Bales and Ron Soodalter. *The Slave Next Door.* University of California Press, Berkeley and Los Angeles, CA, 2009, p. 49.

75 Ibid.

76 Ibid.

77 Ibid.

78 Ibid.

79 Ibid.

80 Ronnie Greene. "A Crop of Abuse." *Miami Herald*, September 1, 2003. http://www.miamiherald.com/2003/09/01/56983/a-crop-of-abuse.html
81 Ibid.
82 Kevin Bales and Ron Soodalter. *The Slave Next Door.* University of California Press, Berkeley and Los Angeles, CA, 2009, p. 49.
83 *"Dying to Leave."* Wide Angle special, PBS, 2003.
84 Ronnie Greene. "A Crop of Abuse." *Miami Herald*, September 1, 2003. http://www.miamiherald.com/2003/09/01/56983/a-crop-of-abuse.html
85 Ibid.
86 Ibid.
87 Kevin Bales and Ron Soodalter. *The Slave Next Door.* University of California Press, Berkeley and Los Angeles, CA, 2009, p. 49.
88 Ibid., p. 50.
89 Ibid.
90 http://www.latinamericanstudies.org/immigration/farmhands-bosses.htm
91 Kevin Bales and Ron Soodalter. *The Slave Next Door.* University of California Press, Berkeley and Los Angeles, CA, 2009, p. 50.
92 Ibid.
93 http://www.warriorsfortruth.com/illegal-alien-fruit-pickers.html
94 Ronnie Greene. "A Crop of Abuse." *Miami Herald*, September 1, 2003 http://www.miamiherald.com/2003/09/01/56983/a-crop-of-abuse.html
95 Ibid.
96 Ibid.
97 Ibid.
98 Ibid.
99 Ibid.
100 http://www.eticafairtrade.com/fairtrade_qanda/
101 http://www.notforsalecampaign.org/about/staff/
102 David Batstone, interview with author, September 22, 2010.
103 www.msnbc.msn.com/id/28415693/ns/us_news-life/
104 Mary A. Fischer. "The Slave in the Garage." *Reader's Digest*, May 2008. http://www.rd.com/your-america-inspiring-people-and-stories/slave-in-the-garage/article55737.html
105 Ibid.
106 http://www.msnbc.msn.com/id/28415693/
107 Rukmini Callimachi. "Child Maid Trafficking Spreads from Africa to US." *Truthout*, December 28, 2008. http://www.truth-out.org/1229080
108 Mary A. Fischer. "The Slave in the Garage." *Reader's Digest*, May 2008. http://www.rd.com/your-america-inspiring-people-and-stories/slave-in-the-garage/article55737.html
109 Ibid.
110 http://www.heraldnet.com/article/20090102/NEWS02/701029924

111 Ibid.

112 Yvette Cabrera. "Child Trafficking Victim Speaks Out." *The Orange County Register*, September 14, 2009. http://www.ocregister.com/articles/hall-211109-trafficking-pertierra.html?pic=1

113 "2006 Trafficking in Persons Report." U.S. Department of State. June 2004. http://www.state.gov/documents/organization/34158.pdf

114 "Charito," interview with author, July 19, 2010.

115 "Eight Arrested in RICO for Visa Fraud, Human Trafficking Conspiracy." May 27, 2009. http://www.ice.gov/news/releases/0905/090527kansascity.htm

116 "Maria Alvarez," interview with author, June 21, 2010.

117 Kevin Bales and Ron Soodalter. *The Slave Next Door*. University of California Press, Berkeley and Los Angeles, CA, 2009, p.165.

118 Demsey, Amy. "Suburban Slavery." *Tusk: The Student Magazine of Cal State Fullerton*, http://tuskmagazine.fullerton.edu/slavery.html

119 Ibid.

120 http://actioncenter.polarisproject.org/index.php?option=com_content&view=article&id=192

121 Matthew 10:16 (Today's New International Version).

122 http://www.salvationarmyusa.org

123 http://www.salvationarmyusa.org/usn/www_usn_2.nsf/vw-dynamic-index/24BBD27490F31F0085257440006B6A93?Opendocument

124 http://www.sharedhope.org/Portals/0/Documents/demand_us.pdf

125 http://www.acf.hhs.gov/trafficking/about/fact_sex.html

126 Ibid.

127 Ibid.

128 http://www.theorator.com/bills109/hr2012.html

129 Anonymous interview with author.

130 Email from anonymous source.

131 Ibid.

132 Gail Dines, *Pornland*, Beacon Press, Boston, MA, 2010.

133 Rebecca Carden. "Panel Discusses Human Trafficking, Sex Work in U.S." http://thebrandeishoot.com/articles/8000

134 Ibid.

135 Janice G. Raymond and Donna M. Hughes. "Sex Trafficking of Women in the United States." March 2001. http://www.uri.edu/artsci/wms/hughes/sex_traff_us.pdf

136 http://www.thepinkcross.org/pinkcross_articles

137 S. Michael Craven." November 8th, 2009. http://www.dakotavoice.com/2009/11/the-secret-war-within-the-church/

138 Ted Roberts. *Pure Desire*. Regal, 2008. http://www.puredesire.org/media/willow_v13_i3_p20-23.pdf

139 "Porn Profits: Corporate America's Secret." May 27, 2004. http://abcnews.go.com/Primetime/story?id=132370&page=1

140 Dustin Kass. "Porn Ban: Winona County Adopts 'Clean Hotel' Policy." *Winona Daily News,* September 8, 2010. http://www.winonadailynews.com/news/local/article_b669f574-bb01-11df-87e7-001cc4c002e0.html

141 Written Testimony of Ernie Allen, President & Chief Executive Officer, National Center for Missing & Exploited Children for the U.S. House of Representatives Subcommittee on Crime, Terrorism and Homeland Security Committee on the Judiciary on 'Domestic Minor Sex Trafficking', Washington DC , September 15, 2010. http://www.missingkids.com/missingkids/servlet/NewsEventServlet?LanguageCountry=en_US&PageId=4339

142 http://www.humantrafficking.org/updates/423

143 Adrienne Sanders. "The City Killed Tiffany Mason: Part 1." *San Francisco Examiner*, May 2002. http://groups.yahoo.com/group/hlf/message/3608

144 Adrienne Sanders. "Poster Child for Broken Promises: Part 5." *San Francisco Examiner*, May 2002. http://groups.yahoo.com/group/hlf/message/3643

145 Adrienne Sanders. "The City Killed Tiffany Mason: Part 1." San Francisco Examiner, May 2002. http://groups.yahoo.com/group/hlf/message/3608

146 Ibid.

147 Adrienne Sanders. "A City Pimp with Big Connections: Part 3." *San Francisco Examiner*, May 2002. http://groups.yahoo.com/group/hlf/message/3607

148 Ibid.

149 http://www.justice.gov/criminal/ceos/prostitution.html

150 Adrienne Sanders. "The City Killed Tiffany Mason: Part 1." *San Francisco Examiner*, May 2002. http://groups.yahoo.com/group/hlf/message/3608

151 Ibid.

152 Adrienne Sanders. "Poster Child for Broken Promises: Part 5." *San Francisco Examiner*, May 2002. http://groups.yahoo.com/group/hlf/message/3643

153 Adrienne Sanders. "Poster Child for Broken Promises: Part 5." *San Francisco Examiner*, May 2002. http://groups.yahoo.com/group/hlf/message/3643

154 Adrienne Sanders. "The City Killed Tiffany Mason: Part 1." San Francisco Examiner, May 2002. http://groups.yahoo.com/group/hlf/message/3608

155 Adrienne Sanders,."Pimps Thrive and Girls Die: Part 4." *San Francisco Examiner*, May 2002. http://groups.yahoo.com/group/hlf/message/3632

156 Adrienne Sanders. "A City Pimp with Big Connections: Part 3." *San Francisco Examiner*, May 2002. http://groups.yahoo.com/group/hlf/message/3607

157 Adrienne Sanders. "Pimps Thrive and Girls Die: Part 4." *San Francisco Examiner*, May 2002. http://groups.yahoo.com/group/hlf/message/3632

158 Adrienne Sanders. "Poster Child for Broken Promises: Part 5." *San Francisco Examiner*, May 2002. http://groups.yahoo. com/group/hlf/message/3643

159 Adrienne Sanders. "The City Killed Tiffany Mason: Part 1." *San Francisco Examiner*, May 2002. http://groups.yahoo.com/group/hlf/message/3608

160 Adrienne Sanders. "The City Killed Tiffany Mason: Part 1." *San Francisco Examiner*, May 2002. http://groups.yahoo.com/group/hlf/message/3608

161 Adrienne Sanders. "Poster Child for Broken Promises: Part 5." *San Francisco Examiner*, May 2002. http://groups.yahoo. com/group/hlf/message/3643

162 Adrienne Sanders. "Pimps Thrive and Girls Die: Part 4." *San Francisco Examiner*, May 2002. http://groups.yahoo.com/group/hlf/message/3632

163 Adrienne Sanders. "Poster Child for Broken Promises: Part 5." *San Francisco Examiner*, May 2002. http://groups.yahoo. com/group/hlf/message/3643

164 Ibid.

165 Ibid.

166 Ibid.

167 Ibid.

168 Adrienne Sanders. "Pimps Thrive and Girls Die: Part 4." *San Francisco Examiner*, May 2002. http://groups.yahoo.com/group/hlf/message/3632

169 Ibid.

170 Ibid.

171 Ibid.

172 Janice G. Raymond and Donna M. Hughes. "Sex Trafficking of Women in the United States." March 2001. http://www.uri. edu/artsci/wms/hughes/sex_traff_us.pdf

173 Keith Bickford, interview with author, January 14, 2009.

174 http://www.actioncenter.polarisproject.org/the-frontlines/survivor-testimonies/39-testimonies-us/77-testimony%20of%20inez

175 Adrienne Sanders. "The City Killed Tiffany Mason: Part 1." *San Francisco Examiner*, May 2002. http://groups.yahoo.com/group/hlf/message/3608

176 Adrienne Sanders. "Poster Child for Broken Promises: Part 5." San Francisco Examiner, May 2002. http://groups.yahoo. com/group/hlf/message/3643

177 Anonymous interview with author.

178 Douglas Hanks. "South Florida should reap $153 million from Super Bowl." *Miami Herald*, January 1, 2010. http://www.miamiherald. com/1460/story/1453154.html

179 Emanuella Grinberg. "Volunteers Try to Dissuade Young Sex Workers on Super Bowl Weekend." CNN, February 6, 2010. http://www.cnn. com/2010/CRIME/02/06/florida.superbowl.sex.trafficking/index. html?hpt=C1

180 Michael J. Mooney and Gus Garcia-Roberts. "Super Bowl Guide to Sex, Drugs, Gambling, and Living Large in South Florida." *Miami New Times*, February 4, 2010. http://www.miaminewtimes.com/2010-02-04/news/ new-times-super-bowl-xliv-guide-to-sex-drugs-gambling-and-living-large-in-south-florida/

181 Patricia Hynes and Janice G. Raymond. "The Neglected Health Consequences of Sex Trafficking in the United States." In J. Sillman and A. Bhattacharjee (Eds). *Policing the National Body: Sex, Race, and Criminalization.* Cambridge: South End, 2002.

182 Melissa Farley. *Prostitution and Trafficking in Nevada.* Prostitution Research and Education, 2007, p. 98.

183 "Victims of Trafficking and Violence Protection Act of 2000: Trafficking in Persons Report." U.S. Department of State 2005. http://www.state. gov/documents/organization/47255.pdf

184 Jonathan Tran. "Sold into Slavery," *The Christian Century*, November 27, 2008, p. 22–26.

185 http://www.readwriteweb. com/archives/advocates_want_craigslist_to_stop_making_money_on.php

186 Janice G. Raymond and Donna M. Hughes. "Sex Trafficking of Women in the United States." March 2001. http://www.uri. edu/artsci/wms/hughes/sex_traff_us.pdf

187 Susan Song. "Global Child Sex Tourism." http://www.yapi.org/ rpchildsextourism.pdf

188 Ibid.

189 Written Testimony of Ernie Allen, President & Chief Executive Officer, National Center for Missing & Exploited Children for the U.S. House of Representatives Subcommittee on Crime, Terrorism and Homeland Security Committee on the Judiciary on 'Domestic Minor Sex Trafficking', Washington D.C., September 15, 2010. http://www.missingkids. com/missingkids/servlet/NewsEventServlet?LanguageCountry=en_ US&PageId=4339

190 Statement of Chris Sweker before the Commission on Security and Cooperation in Europe, United States Helsinki Commission, June 7, 2005. http://www2.fbi.gov/congress/congress05/swecker060705.htm

191 Written Testimony of Ernie Allen, President & Chief Executive Officer, National Center for Missing & Exploited Children for the U.S. House of Representatives Subcommittee on Crime, Terrorism and Homeland Security Committee on the Judiciary on 'Domestic Minor Sex Trafficking',

Washington D.C., September 15, 2010. http://www.missingkids. com/missingkids/servlet/NewsEventServlet?LanguageCountry=en_ US&PageId=4339

192 Anonymous interview with author.

193 Ibid.

194 Brad Dennis, interview with author, January 16, 2009.

195 "Cougar Sighting Reported in Jefferson County." http://www.ktvz.com/ news/22446544/detail.html

196 Anonymous interview with author.

197 "Teen Girls' Stories of Sex Trafficking in U.S." ABC Primetime, February 9, 2006. http://abcnews.go.com/Primetime/story?id=1596778&page=1

198 Vednita Carter and Evelina Giobbe. "Duet: Prostitution, Racism and Feminist Discourse." *Hastings Women's Law Journal* 37:46, 1999.

199 Marianne Wood. *Just a Prostitute.* University of Queensland Press, 1995, p. 55.

200 The Today Show, NBC-TV, December 3, 2008.

201 Anna Rodriguez, interview with author, February 6, 2010.

202 Anonymous interview with author

203 Ibid.

204 Melissa Farley. *Prostitution and Trafficking in Nevada.* Prostitution Research and Education, 2007, p. 181.

205 Ibid., p. 185.

206 http://ag.state.nv.us/victims/Victims%20of%20Crime%20draft%20minu tes%202%2010%2010%20FINAL.pdf

207 Gunilla Ekberg. "The Swedish Law That Prohibits the Purchase of Sexual Services." *Violence Against Women,* October 2004, p. 1187.

208 Mark Lagon. "Taking a Swedish Cue on Prostitution." *Washington Examiner,* November 9, 2009. http://www.washingtonexaminer. com/opinion/columns/OpEd-Contributor/Taking-a-Swedish-cue-on-prostitution-8503882-69523472.html

209 Ibid.

210 "Victims of Trafficking and Violence Protection Act of 2000: Trafficking in Persons Report." U.S. Department of State 2005; http://www.state. gov/documents/organization/47255.pdf

211 Uwe Ewald, Ksenija Turković, *Large-Scale Victimization as a Potential Source of Terrorist Activities,* IOS Press, Amsterdam, Netherlands, 2004, p. 18.

212 The Name is Bond (The Norrmalmstorg Robbery). http://www. nurturingpotential.net/Issue13/Name%20is%20Bond.htm

213 Ibid.

214 Dee L. R. Graham, Edna I. Rawlings, Roberta K. Rigsby. *Loving to Survive: Sexual Terror, Men's Violence, and Women's Lives.* New York University Press, 1994, p. 2.

215 Ibid., p. 1.

216 "The Peace FAQ: The Stockholm Syndrome." http://www.peacefaq.com/stockholm.html

217 http://www.indopedia.org/Norrmalmstorg_robbery.html

218 http://www.statemaster.com/encyclopedia/Norrmalmstorg-robbery

219 Dee L. R. Graham, Edna I. Rawlings, Roberta K. Rigsby. *Loving to Survive: Sexual Terror, Men's Violence, and Women's Lives.* New York University Press, 1994, p. 10.

220 Dee L. R. Graham, Edna I. Rawlings, Roberta K. Rigsby. *Loving to Survive: Sexual Terror, Men's Violence, and Women's Lives.* New York University Press, 1994, p. 5.

221 Ibid., p. 6.

222 Ibid., p. 7.

223 Ibid.

224 Ibid., p. 9.

225 Ibid., p. 10.

226 Ibid.

227 Ibid., p. 11.

228 Ibid., p. 11.

229 Joseph M Carver, PhD. "Love and Stockholm Syndrome: The Mystery of Loving an Abuser (Part 1)."
http://counsellingresource.com/quizzes/stockholm/

230 "Shawn Hornbeck: Jaycee Dugard Brainwashed, in Shock," September 4, 2009.
http://www.people.com/people/news/category/0,,personsTax:
ShawnHornbeck,00.html

231 http://www.newworldencyclopedia.org/entry/Harriet_Tubman

232 Janice G. Raymond and Donna M. Hughes. "Sex Trafficking of Women in the United States." March 2001. http://www.uri.edu/artsci/wms/hughes/sex_traff_us.pdf

233 Melissa Farley. *Prostitution and Trafficking in Nevada.* Prostitution Research and Education, 2007, p. 32.

234 *Diagnostic and Statistical Manual of Mental Disorders: DSM-IV.* American Psychiatric Association: Washington, DC, 1994.

235 Ibid.

236 Rachel Marcus. "Confessions of a Teenage Prostitute." *The Portland Mercury,* September 3, 2009. http://www.portlandmercury.com/portland/confessions-of-a-former-teen-rostitute/Content?oid=1623030

237 Ibid.

238 Ibid.

239 Ibid.

240 Ian Urbina. "For Runaways, Sex Buys Survival." *New York Times*, October 26, 2009. http://www.nytimes.com/2009/10/27/us/27runaways. html?_r=2&hp

241 "Teen Girls' Stories of Sex Trafficking in the US." ABC Primetime, February 9, 2006.

242 http://www.childrenofthenight.org/blog/?p=69

243 Judith Lewis Herman. *Trauma and Recovery: The Aftermath of Violence—from Domestic Abuse to Political Terror.* Basic Books, 1997, p. 92-93.

244 Amanda Kloer. "New Study: Most Pimps Were Trafficked, Abused As Children." *End Human Trafficking.* September 20, 2010. http://humantrafficking.change.org/blog/view/new_study_most_pimps_were_trafficked_abused_as_children

245 "Jason Foster" interview with author.

246 Unpublished Manuscript.

247 http://en.wikipedia.org/wiki/It's_Hard_out_Here_for_a_Pimp

248 http://www.mtv.com/shows/pimp_my_ride/season_5/series.jhtml

249 "Hidden Slaves: Forced Labor in the United States." A report by Free the Slaves (Washington, DC) and Human Rights Center (University of California at Berkeley), September 2004. http://www.law.berkeley.edu/files/hiddenslaves_report.pdf

250 Anonymous interview with author.

251 Brad Dennis, interview with author, January 16, 2009.

252 Ibid.

253 Anonymous interview with author.

254 James 5:16 (Today's New International Version).

255 Hebrews 7:25 (Today's New International Version).

256 Shauna Newell, interview with author, January 15, 2010.

257 Ibid.

258 Brad Dennis, interview with author, January 16, 2009.

259 http://www.ekklesia.co.uk/node/6573

260 Keith Bickford, interview with author, January 14, 2009.

261 Global Forum on Human Trafficking, Carlsbad, CA, October 8, 2

262 Kevin Bales. *Disposable People.* University of California Press, Berkeley and Los Angeles, 1999, p. 8.

263 Matthew 17:20, 21 (Today's New International Version).

264 http://actioncenter.polarisproject.org/index.php?option=com_content&view=article&id=192

About the Author

Nita Belles has worked with victims/survivors of domestic violence for many years, specializing in working with churches and related faith issues. Presently, as the Central Oregon Regional Coordinator for Oregonians Against Trafficking Humans (OATH), which is an extension of the Oregon Human Trafficking Task Force, she focuses on helping victims/survivors of human trafficking and raising awareness about modern-day slavery.

Nita began studying about human trafficking and slavery in 2006. The more she studied, the more she knew she couldn't sit on the sidelines while these atrocities were taking place all over the world, including in her own backyard.

As she networks with other national and international abolitionist organizations, she brings to the table a deep understanding of a broad scope of women's issues, as well as a compassion for victims and a determination to link arms with other abolitionists in order to end modern-day slavery.

Nita has worked for more than twenty years in business. Also, a former Associate Pastor, she holds a Master's Degree in Theology with a concentration in Women's Concerns.

In her leisure times, she loves being with her family. She is an avid Major League Baseball fan and also enjoys fishing, hiking, biking, snowshoeing, and enjoying all the beauty that Central Oregon has to offer.

Nita is available to present to groups everywhere to heighten awareness, answer questions and help stop human trafficking or modern-day slavery. She has an enthusiasm for life and is known as a powerful motivator who will impact any group.

Contact Nita Belles at: InOurBackyardBook@gmail.com

CPSIA information can be obtained at www.ICGtesting.com
Printed in the USA
LVOW06s0152031113

359647LV00001BA/6/P